Algorithms and Data Structures

Algorithms and Data Structures

Dr. Rajendra Biswal

ABD PUBLISHERS
Jaipur ■ New Delhi

ABD PUBLISHERS

Regd. Off. "Bony Residency", Gate No. 2
Opp. Tilak Public School, Vishweswariya Nagar,
Gopalpura Road, Jaipur - 302018, India
Ph: 0141 - 2761280, Telefax: 2761381
Email: abdpublishersjpr@gmail.com

Delhi Office: 102, 1st Floor, Satyam House,
4327/3, Ansari Road, Darya Ganj,
New Delhi - 110002, India
Ph: 011-45652440

visit us: www.oxfordbookcompany.com

Distributed By
KEYA INTERNATIONAL PRESS LLP
E-mail: keyainternationalpressllp@gmail.com

Published in India, 2026

ISBN : 978-81-19343-44-7

Typeset by Shivangi Computer, Jaipur

Printed and bound in India by Thomson Press Ltd.,
New Delhi

Contents

Preface

Algorithm is a formal set of instructions that can be followed to perform a specific task, such as a mathematical formula or a set of instructions in a computer program. Data structure implies an organization of information, usually in memory, for better algorithm efficiency, such as queue, stack, linked list, heap, dictionary, and tree, or conceptual unity, such as the name and address of a person. It may include redundant information, such as length of the list or number of nodes in a sub-tree or external memory data structure, passive data structure, active data structure, persistent data structure, recursive data structure. Most data structures have associated algorithms to perform operations, such as search, insert or balance that maintain the properties of the data structure.

This publication titled, "Algorithms and Data Structures" gives an introduction to algorithm with focus on their characterizations and examples. It also covers other aspects of algorithm such as abstract machine, algorithm design and algorithm engineering. Special emphasis lies on algorithmic efficiency, algorithmic synthesis and program optimization. The dimensions of algorithm trading and computer programme profiling are described. This publication attempts towards creating an understanding the theory of computation and partial function. The theory and model of computation, computability and its partial functions are discussed. Focus also lies on empirical algorithmic and medical algorithm. An introductory overview of data structure and concurrent data structure is provided. Focus also lies on data collection, container and data model, linked data structure and persistent data structure. This publication gives list of terms relating to algorithms and data structures; timeline of algorithms; and list of data structures. Bibliography and glossary are given.

—Dr. Rajendra Biswal

1

Introduction to Algorithm: Characterizations and Examples

ALGORITHM

In mathematics and computer science, an algorithm is an effective method expressed as a finite list of well-defined instructions for calculating a function. Algorithms are used for calculation, data processing, and automated reasoning. Starting from an initial state and initial input (perhaps null), the instructions describe a computation that, when executed, will proceed through a finite number of well-defined successive states, eventually producing "output" and terminating at a final ending state. The transition from one state to the next is not necessarily deterministic; some algorithms, known as randomized algorithms, incorporate random input. A partial formalization of the concept began with attempts to solve the Entscheidungsproblem (the "decision problem") posed by David Hilbert in 1928. Subsequent formalizations were framed as attempts to define "effective calculability" or "effective method"; those formalizations included the Gödel–Herbrand–Kleene recursive functions of 1930, 1934 and 1935, Alonzo Church's lambda calculus of 1936, Emil Post's "Formulation 1" of 1936, and Alan Turing's Turing machines of 1936–7 and 1939.

Why Algorithms are Necessary?

While there is no generally accepted *formal* definition

of "algorithm," an informal definition could be "a set of rules that precisely defines a sequence of operations." For some people, a programme is only an algorithm if it stops eventually; for others, a programme is only an algorithm if it stops before a given number of calculation steps.

A prototypical example of an algorithm is Euclid's algorithm to determine the maximum common divisor of two integers; an example (there are others) is described by the flow chart above and as an example in a later section. Boolos & Jeffrey (1974, 1999) offer an informal meaning of the word in the following quotation:

> No human being can write fast enough, or long enough, or small enough ("smaller and smaller without limit ...you'd be trying to write on molecules, on atoms, on electrons") to list all members of an enumerably infinite set by writing out their names, one after another, in some notation. But humans can do something equally useful, in the case of certain enumerably infinite sets: They can give explicit instructions for determining the *n*th member of the set, for arbitrary finite *n*. Such instructions are to be given quite explicitly, in a form in which they could be followed by a computing machine, or by a human who is capable of carrying out only very elementary operations on symbols

The term "enumerably infinite" means "countable using integers perhaps extending to infinity." Thus Boolos and Jeffrey are saying that an algorithm implies instructions for a process that "creates" output integers from an *arbitrary* "input" integer or integers that, in theory, can be chosen from 0 to infinity. Thus an algorithm can be an algebraic equation such as y = m + n — two arbitrary "input variables" m and n that produce an output y. But various authors' attempts to define the notion indicate that the word implies much more than this, something on the order of (for the addition example):

> Precise instructions (in language understood by "the computer") for a fast, efficient, "good" process that specifies the "moves" of "the computer" (machine or human, equipped with the necessary internally contained information and capabilities) to find, decode, and then process arbitrary input integers/symbols m and n, symbols + and = ... and "effectively" produce, in a "reasonable" time, output-integer y at a specified place and in a specified format.

The concept of *algorithm* is also used to define the notion of decidability. That notion is central for explaining how formal systems come into being starting from a small set of axioms and rules. In logic, the time that an algorithm requires to complete cannot be measured, as it is not apparently related with our customary physical dimension. From such uncertainties, that characterize ongoing work, stems the unavailability of a definition of *algorithm* that suits both concrete (in some sense) and abstract usage of the term.

Formalization

Algorithms are essential to the way computers process data. Many computer programmes contain algorithms that specify the specific instructions a computer should perform (in a specific order) to carry out a specified task, such as calculating employees' paychecks or printing students' report cards. Thus, an algorithm can be considered to be any sequence of operations that can be simulated by a Turing-complete system. Authors who assert this thesis include Minsky (1967), Savage (1987) and Gurevich (2000):

> Minsky: "But we will also maintain, with Turing . . . that any procedure which could "naturally" be called effective, can in fact be realized by a (simple) machine. Although this may seem extreme, the arguments . . . in its favour are hard to refute".

> Gurevich: "...Turing's informal argument in favour

> of his thesis justifies a stronger thesis: every algorithm can be simulated by a Turing machine ... according to Savage [1987], an algorithm is a computational process defined by a Turing machine".

Typically, when an algorithm is associated with processing information, data is read from an input source, written to an output device, and/or stored for further processing. Stored data is regarded as part of the internal state of the entity performing the algorithm. In practice, the state is stored in one or more data structures. For some such computational process, the algorithm must be rigorously defined: specified in the way it applies in all possible circumstances that could arise. That is, any conditional steps must be systematically dealt with, case-by-case; the criteria for each case must be clear (and computable). Because an algorithm is a precise list of precise steps, the order of computation will always be critical to the functioning of the algorithm. Instructions are usually assumed to be listed explicitly, and are described as starting "from the top" and going "down to the bottom", an idea that is described more formally by *flow of control*. So far, this discussion of the formalization of an algorithm has assumed the premises of imperative programming. This is the most common conception, and it attempts to describe a task in discrete, "mechanical" means. Unique to this conception of formalized algorithms is the assignment operation, setting the value of a variable. It derives from the intuition of "memory" as a scratchpad. There is an example below of such an assignment. For some alternate conceptions of what constitutes an algorithm see functional programming and logic programming.

Termination

Some writers restrict the definition of *algorithm* to procedures that eventually finish. In such a category Kleene places the "*decision procedure* or *decision method* or *algorithm* for the question". Others, including Kleene, include procedures that could run forever without stopping; such a procedure has been called a "computational method" or "*calculation procedure* or *algorithm* (and hence a *calculation problem*) in relation to a general question which requires for an answer, not yes or no, but the exhibiting of some object". Minsky makes the pertinent observation, in regards to determining whether an algorithm will eventually terminate (from a particular starting state): But if the length of the process isn't known in advance, then "trying" it may not be decisive, because if the process does go on forever—then at no time will we ever be sure of the answer. As it happens, no other method can do any better, as was shown by Alan Turing with his celebrated result on the undecidability of the so-called halting problem. There is no algorithmic procedure for determining whether or not arbitrary algorithms terminate from given starting states. The analysis of algorithms for their likelihood of termination is called termination analysis.

See the examples of (im-) "proper" subtraction at partial function for more about what can happen when an algorithm fails for certain of its input numbers—e.g., (i) non-termination, (ii) production of "junk" (output in the wrong format to be considered a number) or no number(s) at all (halt ends the computation with no output), (iii) wrong number(s), or (iv) a combination of these. Kleene proposed that the production of "junk" or failure to produce a number is solved by having the algorithm detect these instances and produce e.g., an error message (he suggested "0"), or preferably, force the algorithm into an endless loop. Davis (1958) does this to his subtraction algorithm—he fixes his algorithm in a second example so that it is proper subtraction and it terminates. Along with the logical outcomes "true" and "false" Kleene (1952) also proposes the use of a third logical symbol "u" — undecided — thus an algorithm will always produce *something* when confronted with a "proposition". The problem of wrong answers must be solved with an independent "proof" of the algorithm e.g., using induction: We normally require auxiliary evidence for this [that the algorithm correctly defines a mu recursive function], e.g, in the form of an inductive proof that, for each argument value, the computation terminates with a unique value.

Expressing Algorithms

Algorithms can be expressed in many kinds of notation, including natural languages, pseudocode, flowcharts, programming languages or control tables (processed by interpreters). Natural language expressions of algorithms tend to be verbose and ambiguous, and are rarely used for complex or technical algorithms. Pseudocode, flowcharts and control tables are structured ways to express algorithms that avoid many of the ambiguities common in natural language statements, while remaining independent of a particular implementation language. Programming languages are primarily intended for expressing algorithms in a form that can be executed by a computer, but are often used as a way to define or document algorithms. There is a wide variety of representations possible and one can express a given Turing machine programme as a sequence of machine tables as flowcharts, or as a form of rudimentary machine code or assembly code called "sets of quadruples". Sometimes it is helpful in the description of an algorithm to supplement small "flow charts" (state diagrams) with natural-language and/or arithmetic expressions written inside "block diagrams" to summarize what the "flow charts" are accomplishing. Representations of algorithms are generally classed into three accepted levels of Turing machine description:

- 1 High-level description:
  "...prose to describe an algorithm, ignoring the implementation details. At this level we do not need to mention how the machine manages its tape or head."
- 2 Implementation description:

"...prose used to define the way the Turing machine uses its head and the way that it stores data on its tape. At this level we do not give details of states or transition function."

- 3 Formal description:
  Most detailed, "lowest level", gives the Turing machine's "state table".

Implementation

Most algorithms are intended to be implemented as computer programmes. However, algorithms are also implemented by other means, such as in a biological neural network (for example, the human brain implementing arithmetic or an insect looking for food), in an electrical circuit, or in a mechanical device.

Computer Algorithms

In computer systems, an algorithm is basically an instance of logic written in software by software developers to be effective for the intended "target" computer(s), in order for the target machines to produce *output* from given *input* (perhaps null). "Elegant" (compact) programmes, "good" (fast) programmes : The notion of "simplicity and elegance" appears informally in Knuth and precisely in Chaitin:

> Knuth: ". . .we want *good* algorithms in some loosely defined aesthetic sense. One criterion . . . is the length of time taken to perform the algorithm . . .. Other criteria are adaptability of the algorithm to computers, its simplicity and elegance, etc"
>
> Chaitin: " . . . a programme is 'elegant,' by which I mean that it's the smallest possible programme for producing the output that it does"
>
> Chaitin prefaces his definition with: "I'll show you can't prove that a programme is 'elegant'" — such a proof would solve the Halting problem (ibid).

Algorithm versus function computable by an algorithm: For a given function multiple algorithms may exist. This will be true, even without expanding the available instruction set available to the programmer. Rogers observes that "It is . . . important to distinguish between the notion of *algorithm*, i.e. procedure and the notion of *function computable by algorithm*, i.e. mapping yielded by procedure. The same function may have several different algorithms". Unfortunately there may be a tradeoff between goodness (speed) and elegance (compactness) — an elegant programme may take more steps to complete a computation than one less elegant. An example of using Euclid's algorithm will be shown below. Computers (and computors), models of computation: A computer (or human "computor") is a restricted type of machine, a "discrete deterministic mechanical device" that blindly follows its instructions. Melzak's and Lambek's primitive models reduced this notion to four elements: (i) discrete, distinguishable *locations*, (ii) discrete, indistinguishable *counters* (iii) an agent, and (iv) a list of instructions that are *effective* relative to the capability of the agent.

Minsky describes a more congenial variation of Lambek's "abacus" model in his "Very Simple Bases for Computability". Minsky's machine proceeds sequentially through its five (or six depending on how one counts) instructions unless either a conditional IF - THEN GOTO or an unconditional GOTO changes programme flow out of sequence. Besides HALT, Minsky's machine includes three *assignment* (replacement, substitution) operations: ZERO, SUCCESSOR, and DECREMENT. Rarely will a programmer have to write "code" with such a limited instruction set. But Minsky shows (as do Melzak and Lambek) that his machine is Turing complete with only four general *types* of instructions: conditional GOTO, unconditional GOTO, assignment/ replacement/substitution, and HALT. Simulation of an algorithm: computer(computor) language: Knuth advises the reader that "the best way to learn an algorithm is to try it . . . immediately take pen and paper and work through an example". But what about a simulation or execution of the real thing? The programmer must translate the algorithm into a language that the simulator/computer/computor can *effectively* execute. Stone gives an example of this: when computing the roots of a quadratic equation the computor must know how to take a square root. If they don't then for the algorithm to be effective it must provide a set of rules for extracting a square root.

This means that the programmer must know a "language" that is effective relative to the target computing agent (computer/computor). But what model should be used for the simulation? Van Emde Boas observes "even if we base complexity theory on abstract instead of concrete machines, arbitrariness of the choice of a model remains. It is at this point that the notion of *simulation* enters". When speed is being measured, the instruction set matters. For example, the subprogramme in Euclid's algorithm to compute the remainder would execute much faster if the programmer had a "modulus" (division) instruction available rather than just subtraction (or worse: just Minsky's "decrement"). Structured programming, canonical structures: Per the Church-Turing thesis any algorithm can be computed by a model known to be Turing complete, and per Minsky's demonstrations Turing completeness requires only four instruction types—conditional GOTO, unconditional GOTO, assignment, HALT. Kemeny and Kurtz observe that while "undisciplined" use of unconditional GOTOs and conditional IF-THEN GOTOs can result in "spaghetti code" a programmer can write structured programmes using these instructions; on the other hand "it is also possible, and not too hard, to write badly structured programmes in a structured language".

Tausworthe augments the three Böhm-Jacopini canonical structures: SEQUENCE, IF-THEN-ELSE, and WHILE-DO, with two more: DO-WHILE and CASE. An additional benefit of a structured programme will be one that lends itself to proofs of correctness using mathematical induction. Canonical flowchart symbols: The graphical aide called a flowchart offers a way to describe and document an algorithm (and a computer programme of one). Like programme flow of a Minsky machine, a flowchart always starts at the top of a page and proceeds down. Its primary symbols are only 4: the directed arrow showing programme flow, the rectangle (SEQUENCE, GOTO), the diamond (IF-THEN-ELSE), and the dot (OR-tie). The Böhm-Jacopini canonical structures are made of these primitive shapes. Sub-structures can "nest" in rectangles but only if a single exit occurs from the superstructure. The symbols and their use to build the canonical structures are shown in the diagram.

Examples

Sorting Example

One of the simplest algorithms is to find the largest number in an (unsorted) list of numbers. The solution necessarily requires looking at every number in the list, but only once at each. From this follows a simple algorithm, which can be stated in a high-level description English prose, as: High-level description:

1. Assume the first item is largest.
2. Look at each of the remaining items in the list and if it is larger than the largest item so far, make a note of it.
3. The last noted item is the largest in the list when the process is complete.

   (Quasi-)formal description: Written in prose but much closer to the high-level language of a computer programme, the following is the more formal coding of the algorithm.

Euclid's Algorithm

Euclid's algorithm appears as Proposition II in Book VII ("Elementary Number Theory") of his *Elements*. Euclid poses the problem: "Given two numbers not prime to one another, to find their greatest common measure". He defines "A number [to be] a multitude composed of units": a counting number, a positive integer not including 0. And to "measure" is to place a shorter measuring length s successively (q times) along longer length l until the remaining portion r is less than the shorter length s. In modern words, remainder $r = l - q*s$, q being the quotient, or remainder r is the "modulus", the integer-fractional part left over after the division. For Euclid's method to succeed, the starting lengths must satisfy two requirements: (i) the lengths must not be 0, AND (ii) the subtraction must be "proper", a test must guarantee that the smaller of the two numbers is subtracted from the larger (alternately, the two can be equal so their subtraction yields 0). Euclid's original proof adds a third: the two lengths are not prime to one another. Euclid stipulated this so that he could construct a reductio ad absurdum proof that the two numbers' common measure is in fact the *greatest*. While Nicomachus' algorithm is the same as Euclid's, when the numbers are prime to one another it yields the number "1" for their common measure. So to be precise the following is really Nicomachus' algorithm.

Computer (Computor) Language for Euclid's Algorithm

Only a few instruction *types* are required to execute Euclid's algorithm—some logical tests (conditional GOTO), unconditional GOTO, assignment (replacement), and subtraction.

- A *location* is symbolized by upper case letter(s), e.g. S, A, etc.
- The varying quantity (number) in a location will be written in lower case letter(s) and (usually)

associated with the location's name. For example, location L at the start might contain the number $l = 3009$.

How "Elegant" works: In place of an outer "Euclid loop", "Elegant" shifts back and forth between two "co-loops", an A > B loop that computes A •! A - B, and a B d" A loop that computes B •! B - A. This works because, when at last the minuend M is less than or equal to the subtrahend S (Difference = Minuend - Subtrahend), the minuend can become *s* (the new measuring length) and the subtrahend can become the new *r* (the length to be measured); in other words the "sense" of the subtraction reverses.

Testing the Euclid Algorithms

Does an algorithm do what its author wants it to do? A few test cases usually suffice to confirm core functionality. One source uses 3009 and 884. Knuth suggested 40902, 24140. Another interesting case is the two relatively-prime numbers 14157 and 5950. But exceptional cases must be identified and tested. Will "Inelegant" perform properly when R > S, S > R, R = S? Ditto for "Elegant": B > A, A > B, A = B? (Yes to all). What happens when one number is zero, both numbers are zero? ("Inelegant" computes forever in all cases; "Elegant" computes forever when A = 0.) What happens if *negative* numbers are entered?

Fractional numbers? If the input numbers, i.e. the domain of the function computed by the algorithm/ programme, is to include only positive integers including zero, then the failures at zero indicate that the algorithm (and the programme that instantiates it) is a partial function rather than a total function. A notable failure due to exceptions is the Ariane V rocket failure. Proof of programme correctness by use of mathematical induction: Knuth demonstrates the application of mathematical induction to an "extended" version of Euclid's algorithm, and he proposes "a general method applicable to proving the validity of any algorithm". Tausworthe proposes that a measure of the complexity of a programme be the length of its correctness proof.

Measuring and Improving the Euclid Algorithms

Elegance (compactness) versus goodness (speed) : With only 6 core instructions, "Elegant" is the clear winner compared to "Inelegant" at 13 instructions. However, "Inelegant" is *faster* (it arrives at HALT in fewer steps). Algorithm analysis indicates why this is the case: "Elegant" does *two* conditional tests in every subtraction loop, whereas "Inelegant" only does one. As the algorithm (usually) requires many loop-throughs, *on average* much time is wasted doing a "B = 0?" test that is needed only after the remainder is computed. Can the algorithms be improved?: Once the programmer judges a programme "fit" and "effective" — that is, it computes the function intended by its author— then the question becomes, can it be improved? The compactness of "Inelegant" can be improved by the elimination of 5 steps. But Chaitin proved that compacting an algorithm cannot be automated by a generalized algorithm; rather, it can only be done heuristically, i.e. by exhaustive search (examples to be found at Busy beaver), trial and error, cleverness, insight, application of inductive reasoning, etc. Observe that steps 4, 5 and 6 are repeated in steps 11, 12 and 13.

Comparison with "Elegant" provides a hint that these steps together with steps 2 and 3 can be eliminated. This reduces the number of core instructions from 13 to 8, which makes it "more elegant" than "Elegant" at 9 steps. The speed of "Elegant" can be improved by moving the B=0? test outside of the two subtraction loops. This change calls for the addition of 3 instructions (B=0?, A=0?, GOTO). Now "Elegant" computes the example-numbers faster; whether for any given A, B and R, S this is always the case would require a detailed analysis.

Algorithmic Analysis

It is frequently important to know how much of a particular resource (such as time or storage) is theoretically required for a given algorithm. Methods have been developed for the analysis of algorithms to obtain such quantitative answers (estimates); for example, the sorting algorithm above has a time requirement of $O(n)$, using the big O notation with n as the length of the list. At all times the algorithm only needs to remember two values: the largest number found so far, and its current position in the input list. Therefore it is said to have a space requirement of $O(1)$, if the space required to store the input numbers is not counted, or $O(n)$ if it is counted. Different algorithms may complete the same task with a different set of instructions in less or more time, space, or 'effort' than others. For example, a binary search algorithm will usually outperform a brute force sequential search when used for table lookups on sorted lists.

Formal Versus Empirical

The analysis and study of algorithms is a discipline of computer science, and is often practiced abstractly without the use of a specific programming language or implementation. In this sense, algorithm analysis resembles other mathematical disciplines in that it focuses on the underlying properties of the algorithm and not on the specifics of any particular implementation. Usually pseudocode is used for analysis as it is the simplest and most general representation. However, ultimately, most algorithms are usually implemented on particular hardware / software platforms and their algorithmic efficiency is eventually put to the test using real code. Empirical testing is useful because it may uncover unexpected interactions that affect performance. Benchmarks may be used to compare before/after potential improvements to an algorithm after programme optimization.

Classification

There are various ways to classify algorithms, each with its own merits.

By Implementation

One way to classify algorithms is by implementation means.

- Recursion or iteration: A recursive algorithm is one that invokes (makes reference to) itself repeatedly until a certain condition matches, which is a method common to functional programming. Iterative algorithms use repetitive constructs like loops and sometimes additional data structures like stacks to solve the given problems. Some problems are naturally suited for one implementation or the other. For example, towers of Hanoi is well understood in recursive implementation. Every recursive version has an equivalent (but possibly more or less complex) iterative version, and vice versa.
- Logical: An algorithm may be viewed as controlled logical deduction. This notion may be expressed as: Algorithm = logic + control. The logic component expresses the axioms that may be used in the computation and the control component determines the way in which deduction is applied to the axioms. This is the basis for the logic programming paradigm. In pure logic programming languages the control component is fixed and algorithms are specified by supplying only the logic component. The appeal of this approach is the elegant semantics: a change in the axioms has a well defined change in the algorithm.
- Serial or parallel or distributed: Algorithms are usually discussed with the assumption that

computers execute one instruction of an algorithm at a time. Those computers are sometimes called serial computers. An algorithm designed for such an environment is called a serial algorithm, as opposed to parallel algorithms or distributed algorithms. Parallel algorithms take advantage of computer architectures where several processors can work on a problem at the same time, whereas distributed algorithms utilize multiple machines connected with a network. Parallel or distributed algorithms divide the problem into more symmetrical or asymmetrical subproblems and collect the results back together. The resource consumption in such algorithms is not only processor cycles on each processor but also the communication overhead between the processors. Sorting algorithms can be parallelized efficiently, but their communication overhead is expensive. Iterative algorithms are generally parallelizable. Some problems have no parallel algorithms, and are called inherently serial problems.

- Deterministic or non-deterministic: Deterministic algorithms solve the problem with exact decision at every step of the algorithm whereas non-deterministic algorithms solve problems via guessing although typical guesses are made more accurate through the use of heuristics.
- Exact or approximate: While many algorithms reach an exact solution, approximation algorithms seek an approximation that is close to the true solution. Approximation may use either a deterministic or a random strategy. Such algorithms have practical value for many hard problems.
- Quantum algorithm: Quantum algorithm run on a realistic model of quantum computation. The term is usually used for those algorithms which

seem inherently quantum, or use some essential feature of quantum computation such as quantum superposition or quantum entanglement.

By Design Paradigm

Another way of classifying algorithms is by their design methodology or paradigm. There is a certain number of paradigms, each different from the other. Furthermore, each of these categories will include many different types of algorithms. Some commonly found paradigms include:

- Brute-force or exhaustive search. This is the naïve method of trying every possible solution to see which is best.
- Divide and conquer. A divide and conquer algorithm repeatedly reduces an instance of a problem to one or more smaller instances of the same problem (usually recursively) until the instances are small enough to solve easily. One such example of divide and conquer is merge sorting. Sorting can be done on each segment of data after dividing data into segments and sorting of entire data can be obtained in the conquer phase by merging the segments. A simpler variant of divide and conquer is called a decrease and conquer algorithm, that solves an identical subproblem and uses the solution of this subproblem to solve the bigger problem. Divide and conquer divides the problem into multiple subproblems and so the conquer stage will be more complex than decrease and conquer algorithms. An example of decrease and conquer algorithm is the binary search algorithm.
- Dynamic programming. When a problem shows optimal substructure, meaning the optimal solution to a problem can be constructed from optimal solutions to subproblems, and overlapping sub-problems, meaning the same subproblems are used

to solve many different problem instances, a quicker approach called *dynamic programming* avoids recomputing solutions that have already been computed. For example, Floyd–Warshall algorithm, the shortest path to a goal from a vertex in a weighted graph can be found by using the shortest path to the goal from all adjacent vertices. Dynamic programming and memoization go together. The main difference between dynamic programming and divide and conquer is that subproblems are more or less independent in divide and conquer, whereas subproblems overlap in dynamic programming. The difference between dynamic programming and straightforward recursion is in caching or memoization of recursive calls. When subproblems are independent and there is no repetition, memoization does not help; hence dynamic programming is not a solution for all complex problems. By using memoization or maintaining a table of subproblems already solved, dynamic programming reduces the exponential nature of many problems to polynomial complexity.

- The greedy method. A greedy algorithm is similar to a dynamic programming algorithm, but the difference is that solutions to the subproblems do not have to be known at each stage; instead a "greedy" choice can be made of what looks best for the moment. The greedy method extends the solution with the best possible decision (not all feasible decisions) at an algorithmic stage based on the current local optimum and the best decision (not all possible decisions) made in a previous stage. It is not exhaustive, and does not give an accurate answer to many problems. But when it works, it will be the fastest method. The most popular greedy algorithm is finding the minimal spanning tree as given by Huffman Tree, Kruskal, Prim, Sollin.

- Linear programming. When solving a problem using linear programming, specific inequalities involving the inputs are found and then an attempt is made to maximize (or minimize) some linear function of the inputs. Many problems (such as the maximum flow for directed graphs) can be stated in a linear programming way, and then be solved by a 'generic' algorithm such as the simplex algorithm. A more complex variant of linear programming is called integer programming, where the solution space is restricted to the integers.
- Reduction. This technique involves solving a difficult problem by transforming it into a better known problem for which we have (hopefully) asymptotically optimal algorithms. The goal is to find a reducing algorithm whose complexity is not dominated by the resulting reduced algorithm's. For example, one selection algorithm for finding the median in an unsorted list involves first sorting the list (the expensive portion) and then pulling out the middle element in the sorted list (the cheap portion). This technique is also known as *transform and conquer*.
- Search and enumeration. Many problems (such as playing chess) can be modeled as problems on graphs. A graph exploration algorithm specifies rules for moving around a graph and is useful for such problems. This category also includes search algorithms, branch and bound enumeration and backtracking.

1. Randomized algorithms are those that make some choices randomly (or pseudo-randomly); for some problems, it can in fact be proven that the fastest solutions must involve some randomness. There are two large classes of such algorithms:

(a) Monte Carlo algorithms return a correct answer with high-probability. E.g. RP is the subclass of these that run in polynomial time)

(b) Las Vegas algorithms always return the correct answer, but their running time is only probabilistically bound, e.g. ZPP.

2. In optimization problems, heuristic algorithms do not try to find an optimal solution, but an approximate solution where the time or resources are limited. They are not practical to find perfect solutions. An example of this would be local search, tabu search, or simulated annealing algorithms, a class of heuristic probabilistic algorithms that vary the solution of a problem by a random amount. The name "simulated annealing" alludes to the metallurgic term meaning the heating and cooling of metal to achieve freedom from defects. The purpose of the random variance is to find close to globally optimal solutions rather than simply locally optimal ones, the idea being that the random element will be decreased as the algorithm settles down to a solution. Approximation algorithms are those heuristic algorithms that additionally provide some bounds on the error. Genetic algorithms attempt to find solutions to problems by mimicking biological evolutionary processes, with a cycle of random mutations yielding successive generations of "solutions". Thus, they emulate reproduction and "survival of the fittest". In genetic programming, this approach is extended to algorithms, by regarding the algorithm itself as a "solution" to a problem.

By Field of Study

Every field of science has its own problems and needs efficient algorithms. Related problems in one field are often studied together. Some example classes are search algorithms, sorting algorithms, merge algorithms, numerical algorithms, graph algorithms, string algorithms, computational geometric algorithms, combinatorial algorithms, medical algorithms, machine learning, cryptography, data compression algorithms and parsing techniques. Fields tend to overlap with each other, and algorithm advances in one field may improve those of other, sometimes completely unrelated, fields. For example, dynamic programming was invented for optimization of resource consumption in industry, but is now used in solving a broad range of problems in many fields.

By Complexity

Algorithms can be classified by the amount of time they need to complete compared to their input size. There is a wide variety: some algorithms complete in linear time relative to input size, some do so in an exponential amount of time or even worse, and some never halt. Additionally, some problems may have multiple algorithms of differing complexity, while other problems might have no algorithms or no known efficient algorithms. There are also mappings from some problems to other problems. Owing to this, it was found to be more suitable to classify the problems themselves instead of the algorithms into equivalence classes based on the complexity of the best possible algorithms for them. Burgin (2005, p. 24) uses a generalized definition of algorithms that relaxes the common requirement that the output of the algorithm that computes a function must be determined after a finite number of steps. He defines a super-recursive class of algorithms as “a class of algorithms in which it is possible to compute functions not computable by any Turing machine” (Burgin 2005, p. 107). This is closely related to the study of methods of hypercomputation.

Continuous Algorithms

The adjective “continuous” when applied to the word “algorithm” can mean:

1. An algorithm operating on data that represents continuous quantities, even though this data is represented by discrete approximations – such algorithms are studied in numerical analysis; or

2. An algorithm in the form of a differential equation that operates continuously on the data, running on an analog computer.

Legal Issues

Algorithms, by themselves, are not usually patentable. In the United States, a claim consisting solely of simple manipulations of abstract concepts, numbers, or signals does not constitute "processes" (USPTO 2006), and hence algorithms are not patentable (as in Gottschalk v. Benson). However, practical applications of algorithms are sometimes patentable. For example, in Diamond v. Diehr, the application of a simple feedback algorithm to aid in the curing of synthetic rubber was deemed patentable. The patenting of software is highly controversial, and there are highly criticized patents involving algorithms, especially data compression algorithms, such as Unisys' LZW patent. Additionally, some cryptographic algorithms have export restrictions.

Etymology

The word *"Algorithm"* or *"Algorism"* in some other writing versions, comes from the name Al-Khwarizmi (c. 780-850), a Persian mathematician, astronomer, geographer and a scholar in the House of Wisdom in Baghdad, whose name means *"the native of Kharazm"*, a city that was part of the Greater Iran during his era and now is in modern day Uzbekistan He wrote a treatise in Arabic language in the 9th century, which was translated into Latin in the 12th century under the title *Algoritmi de numero Indorum*. This title means "Algoritmi on the numbers of the Indians", where "Algoritmi" was the translator's Latinization of Al-Khwarizmi's name. Al-Khwarizmi was the most widely read mathematician in Europe in the late Middle Ages, primarily through his other book, the Algebra. In late medieval Latin, *algorismus*, the corruption of his name, simply meant the "decimal number system" that is still the meaning of modern English algorism. In 17th century French the word's form, but not its meaning, changed to *algorithme*. English adopted the French very soon afterwards, but it wasn't until the late 19th century that "Algorithm" took on the meaning that it has in modern English.

History: Development of the Notion of "Algorithm"

Discrete and Distinguishable Symbols

Tally-marks: To keep track of their flocks, their sacks of grain and their money the ancients used tallying: accumulating stones or marks scratched on sticks, or making discrete symbols in clay. Through the Babylonian and Egyptian use of marks and symbols, eventually Roman numerals and the abacus evolved (Dilson, p. 16–41). Tally marks appear prominently in unary numeral system arithmetic used in Turing machine and Post–Turing machine computations.

Manipulation of Symbols as "Place Holders" for Numbers: Algebra

The work of the ancient Greek geometers (Euclidean algorithm), Persian mathematician Al-Khwarizmi (from whose name the terms "algorism" and "algorithm" are derived), and Western European mathematicians culminated in Leibniz's notion of the calculus ratiocinator (ca 1680): A good century and a half ahead of his time, Leibniz proposed an algebra of logic, an algebra that would specify the rules for manipulating logical concepts in the manner that ordinary algebra specifies the rules for manipulating numbers.

Mechanical Contrivances with Discrete States

The clock: Bolter credits the invention of the weight-driven clock as "The key invention [of Europe in the Middle Ages]", in particular the verge escapement that provides us with the tick and tock of a mechanical clock. "The accurate automatic machine" led immediately to "mechanical automata" beginning in the 13th century and finally to "computational machines" – the difference engine and analytical engines of Charles Babbage and Countess Ada Lovelace. Logical machines 1870 – Stanley Jevons' "logical abacus" and "logical machine": The technical problem was to reduce Boolean equations when presented in a form similar to what are now known as Karnaugh maps. Jevons (1880) describes first a simple "abacus" of "slips of wood furnished with pins, contrived so that any part or class of the [logical] combinations can be picked out mechanically . . . More recently however I have reduced the system to a completely mechanical form, and have thus embodied the whole of the indirect process of inference in what may be called a Logical Machine" His machine came equipped with "certain moveable wooden rods" and "at the foot are 21 keys like those of a piano [etc] . . .". With this machine he could analyze a "syllogism or any other simple logical argument".

This machine he displayed in 1870 before the Fellows of the Royal Society. Another logician John Venn, however, in his 1881 *Symbolic Logic*, turned a jaundiced eye to this effort: "I have no high estimate myself of the interest or importance of what are sometimes called logical machines ... it does not seem to me that any contrivances at present known or likely to be discovered really deserve the name of logical machines"; see more at Algorithm characterizations. But not to be outdone he too presented "a plan somewhat analogous, I apprehend, to Prof. Jevon's *abacus* ... [And] [a]gain, corresponding to Prof. Jevons's logical machine, the following contrivance may be described. I prefer to call it merely a logical-diagram machine ... but I suppose that it could do very completely all that can be rationally expected of any logical machine". Jacquard loom, Hollerith punch cards, telegraphy and telephony—the electromechanical relay: Bell and Newell (1971) indicate that the Jacquard loom (1801), precursor to Hollerith cards (punch cards, 1887), and "telephone switching technologies" were the roots of a tree leading to the development of the first computers.

By the mid-19th century the telegraph, the precursor of the telephone, was in use throughout the world, its discrete and distinguishable encoding of letters as "dots and dashes" a common sound. By the late 19th century the ticker tape (ca 1870s) was in use, as was the use of Hollerith cards in the 1890 U.S. census. Then came the Teletype (ca. 1910) with its punched-paper use of Baudot code on tape. Telephone-switching networks of electromechanical relays (invented 1835) was behind the work of George Stibitz (1937), the inventor of the digital adding device. As he worked in Bell Laboratories, he observed the "burdensome' use of mechanical calculators with gears. "He went home one evening in 1937 intending to test his idea... When the tinkering was over, Stibitz had constructed a binary adding device". Davis (2000) observes the particular importance of the electromechanical relay (with its two "binary states" *open* and *closed*): It was only with the development, beginning in the 1930s, of electromechanical calculators using electrical relays, that machines were built having the scope Babbage had envisioned."

Mathematics during the 1800s up to the Mid-1900s

Symbols and rules: In rapid succession the mathematics of George Boole (1847, 1854), Gottlob Frege (1879), and Giuseppe Peano (1888–1889) reduced arithmetic to a sequence of symbols manipulated by rules. Peano's *The principles of arithmetic, presented by a new method* (1888) was "the first attempt at an axiomatization of mathematics in a symbolic language". But Heijenoort gives Frege (1879) this kudos: Frege's is "perhaps the most important single work ever written in logic. ... in which we see a " 'formula language', that is a *lingua characterica*, a language written with special symbols, "for pure thought", that is, free from rhetorical embellishments ... constructed from specific symbols that are manipulated according to definite rules". The work of Frege was further simplified and amplified by Alfred North Whitehead and Bertrand Russell in their Principia Mathematica (1910–1913). The paradoxes: At the same time a number of disturbing paradoxes appeared in the literature, in particular the Burali-Forti paradox (1897), the Russell paradox (1902–03), and the Richard Paradox. The resultant considerations led to Kurt Gödel's paper (1931) — he specifically cites the paradox of the liar—that completely reduces rules of recursion to numbers.

Effective calculability: In an effort to solve the Entscheidungsproblem defined precisely by Hilbert in 1928, mathematicians first set about to define what was meant by an "effective method" or "effective calculation" or "effective calculability" (i.e., a calculation that would succeed). In rapid succession the following appeared: Alonzo Church, Stephen Kleene and J.B. Rosser's ë-calculus a finely honed definition of "general recursion" from the work of Gödel acting on suggestions of Jacques Herbrand (cf. Gödel's Princeton lectures of 1934) and subsequent simplifications by Kleene. Church's proof that the Entscheidungsproblem was unsolvable, Emil Post's definition of effective calculability as a worker mindlessly following a list of instructions to move left or right through a sequence of rooms and while there either mark or erase a paper or observe the paper and make a yes-no decision about the next instruction. Alan Turing's proof of that the Entscheidungsproblem was unsolvable by use of his "a-[automatic-] machine" – in effect almost identical to Post's "formulation", J. Barkley Rosser's definition of "effective method" in terms of "a machine". S. C. Kleene's proposal of a precursor to "Church thesis" that he called "Thesis I", and a few years later Kleene's renaming his Thesis "Church's Thesis" and proposing "Turing's Thesis".

Emil Post (1936) and Alan Turing (1936–7, 1939)

Here is a remarkable coincidence of two men not knowing

each other but describing a process of men-as-computers working on computations—and they yield virtually identical definitions. Emil Post (1936) described the actions of a "computer" (human being) as follows:

> "...two concepts are involved: that of a *symbol space* in which the work leading from problem to answer is to be carried out, and a fixed unalterable *set of directions*.

His symbol space would be

> "a two way infinite sequence of spaces or boxes... The problem solver or worker is to move and work in this symbol space, being capable of being in, and operating in but one box at a time.... a box is to admit of but two possible conditions, i.e., being empty or unmarked, and having a single mark in it, say a vertical stroke.
>
> "One box is to be singled out and called the starting point. ...a specific problem is to be given in symbolic form by a finite number of boxes [i.e., INPUT] being marked with a stroke. Likewise the answer [i.e., OUTPUT] is to be given in symbolic form by such a configuration of marked boxes....
>
> "A set of directions applicable to a general problem sets up a deterministic process when applied to each specific problem. This process will terminate only when it comes to the direction of type (C) [i.e., STOP]".

Alan Turing's work preceded that of Stibitz (1937); it is unknown whether Stibitz knew of the work of Turing. Turing's biographer believed that Turing's use of a typewriter-like model derived from a youthful interest: "Alan had dreamt of inventing typewriters as a boy; Mrs. Turing had a typewriter; and he could well have begun by asking himself what was meant by calling a typewriter 'mechanical'". Given the prevalence of Morse code and telegraphy, ticker tape machines, and Teletypes we might conjecture that all were influences. Turing—his model of computation is now called a Turing machine — begins, as did Post, with an analysis of a human computer that he whittles down to a simple set of basic motions and "states of mind". But he continues a step further and creates a machine as a model of computation of numbers. "Computing is normally done by writing certain symbols on paper. We may suppose this paper is divided into squares like a child's arithmetic book....I assume then that the computation is carried out on one-dimensional paper, i.e., on a tape divided into squares. I shall also suppose that the number of symbols which may be printed is finite....

"The behaviour of the computer at any moment is determined by the symbols which he is observing, and his "state of mind" at that moment. We may suppose that there is a bound B to the number of symbols or squares which the computer can observe at one moment. If he wishes to observe more, he must use successive observations. We will also suppose that the number of states of mind which need be taken into account is finite... "Let us imagine that the operations performed by the computer to be split up into 'simple operations' which are so elementary that it is not easy to imagine them further divided". Turing's reduction yields the following: "The simple operations must therefore include:

"(a) Changes of the symbol on one of the observed squares

"(b) Changes of one of the squares observed to another square within L squares of one of the previously observed squares.

"It may be that some of these change necessarily invoke a change of state of mind. The most general single operation must therefore be taken to be one of the following:

"(A) A possible change (a) of symbol together with a possible change of state of mind.

"(B) A possible change (b) of observed squares, together with a possible change of state of mind"

"We may now construct a machine to do the work of this computer".

A few years later, Turing expanded his analysis (thesis, definition) with this forceful expression of it:

> "A function is said to be "effectively calculable" if its values can be found by some purely mechanical process. Although it is fairly easy to get an intuitive grasp of this idea, it is nevertheless desirable to have some more definite, mathematical expressible definition . . . [he discusses the history of the definition pretty much as presented above with respect to Gödel, Herbrand, Kleene, Church, Turing and Post] . . . We may take this statement literally, understanding by a purely mechanical process one which could be carried out by a machine. It is possible to give a mathematical description, in a certain normal form, of the structures of these machines. The development of these ideas leads to the author's definition of a computable function, and to an identification of computability † with effective calculability . . . .

J.B. Rosser (1939) and S.C. Kleene (1943)

J. Barkley Rosser boldly defined an 'effective [mathematical] method' in the following manner (boldface added):

> "'Effective method' is used here in the rather special sense of a method each step of which is precisely determined and which is certain to produce the answer in a finite number of steps. With this special meaning, three different precise definitions have been given to date. [his footnote #5; see discussion immediately below]. The simplest of these to state (due to Post and Turing) says essentially that an effective method of solving certain sets of problems

> exists if one can build a machine which will then solve any problem of the set with no human intervention beyond inserting the question and (later) reading the answer. All three definitions are equivalent, so it doesn't matter which one is used. Moreover, the fact that all three are equivalent is a very strong argument for the correctness of any one." (Rosser 1939:225–6)

Rosser's footnote #5 references the work of (1) Church and Kleene and their definition of ë-definability, in particular Church's use of it in his *An Unsolvable Problem of Elementary Number Theory* (1936); (2) Herbrand and Gödel and their use of recursion in particular Gödel's use in his famous paper *On Formally Undecidable Propositions of Principia Mathematica and Related Systems I* (1931); and (3) Post (1936) and Turing (1936–7) in their mechanism-models of computation. Stephen C. Kleene defined as his now-famous "Thesis I" known as the Church–Turing thesis. But he did this in the following context (boldface in original):

> "12. Algorithmic theories... In setting up a complete algorithmic theory, what we do is to describe a procedure, performable for each set of values of the independent variables, which procedure necessarily terminates and in such manner that from the outcome we can read a definite answer, "yes" or "no," to the question, "is the predicate value true?"" (Kleene 1943:273)

History After 1950

A number of efforts have been directed toward further refinement of the definition of "algorithm", and activity is on-going because of issues surrounding, in particular, foundations of mathematics (especially the Church–Turing thesis) and philosophy of mind (especially arguments around artificial intelligence). For more, see Algorithm characterizations.

ALGORITHM CHARACTERIZATIONS

The word algorithm does not have a generally accepted definition. Researchers are actively working in formalizing this term. This study will present some of the "characterizations" of the notion of "algorithm" in more detail.

The Problem of Definition

There is no generally accepted definition of algorithm. Over the last 200 years the definition has become more complicated and detailed as researchers have tried to pin down the term. Indeed there may be more than one type of "algorithm". But most agree that algorithm has something to do with defining generalized processes for the creation of "output" integers from other "input" integers — "input parameters" arbitrary and infinite in extent, or limited in extent but still variable—by the manipulation of distinguishable symbols (counting numbers) with finite collections of rules that a person can perform with paper and pencil. The most common number-manipulation schemes—both in formal mathematics and in routine life—are: (1) the recursive functions calculated by a person with paper and pencil, and (2) the Turing machine or its Turing equivalents—the primitive register machine or "counter machine" model, the Random Access Machine model (RAM), the Random access stored programme machine model (RASP) and its functional equivalent "the computer".

The reader is probably unfamiliar with the notion of a "recursive function". But when we are doing "arithmetic" we are really calculating by the use of "recursive functions" in the shorthand algorithms we learned in grade-school, for example, adding and subtracting. The proofs that every "recursive function" we can *calculate by hand* we can *compute by machine* and vice versa—note the usage of the words *calculate* versus *compute* — is remarkable. But this equivalence together with the *thesis* (hypothesis, unproven assertion) that this includes *every* calculation/computation indicates why so much emphasis has been placed upon the use of Turing-equivalent machines in the definition of specific algorithms, and why the definition of "algorithm" itself often refers back to "the Turing machine". This is discussed in more detail under Stephen Kleene's characterization. The following are summaries of the more famous characterizations (Kleene, Markov, Knuth) together with those that introduce novel elements—elements that further expand the definition or contribute to a more precise definition.

Chomsky Hierarchy

There is more consensus on the "characterization" of the notion of "simple algorithm". All algorithms need to be specified in a formal language, and the "simplicity notion" arises from the simplicity of the language. The Chomsky (1956) hierarchy is a containment hierarchy of classes of formal grammars that generate formal languages. It is used for classifying of programming languages and abstract machines. From the *Chomsky hierarchy* perspective, if the algorithm can be specified on a simpler language (than unrestricted), it can be characterized by this kind of language, else it is a typical "unrestricted algorithm". Examples: a "general purpose" macro language, like M4 is unrestricted (Turing complete), but the C preprocessor macro language is not, so any algorithm expressed in *C preprocessor* is a "simple algorithm".

Characterizations of the Notion of "Algorithm"

1881 John Venn's negative reaction to W. Stanley Jevons's Logical Machine of 1870 In early 1870 W. Stanley Jevons presented a "Logical Machine" (Jevons 1880:200) for analyzing a syllogism or other logical form e.g. an argument reduced to a Boolean equation. By means of what Couturat (1914) called a "sort of *logical piano* [,] ...

the equalities which represent the premises ... are "played" on a keyboard like that of a typewriter. ... When all the premises have been "played", the panel shows only those constituents whose sum is equal to 1, that is, ... its logical whole. This mechanical method has the advantage over VENN's geometrical method..." (Couturat 1914:75). For his part John Venn, a logician contemporary to Jevons, was less than thrilled, opining that "it does not seem to me that any contrivances at present known *or likely to be discovered* really deserve the name of logical machines" (italics added, Venn 1881:120). But of historical use to the developing notion of "algorithm" is his explanation for his negative reaction with respect to a machine that "may subserve a really valuable purpose by enabling us to avoid otherwise inevitable labor":

(1) "There is, first, the statement of our data in accurate logical language",

(2) "Then secondly, we have to throw these statements into a form fit for the engine to work with — in this case the reduction of each proposition to its elementary denials",

(3) "Thirdly, there is the combination or further treatment of our premises after such reduction,"

(4) "Finally, the results have to be interpreted or read off. This last generally gives rise to much opening for skill and sagacity."

He concludes that "I cannot see that any machine can hope to help us except in the third of these steps; so that it seems very doubtful whether any thing of this sort really deserves the name of a logical engine."(Venn 1881:119-121).

1943, 1952 Stephen Kleene's Characterization

This section is longer and more detailed than the others because of its importance to the topic: Kleene was the first to propose that *all* calculations/computations—of *every* sort, the *totality* of—can *equivalently* be (i) *calculated* by use of five "primitive recursive operators" plus one special operator called the mu-operator, or be (ii) *computed* by the actions of a Turing machine or an equivalent model. Furthermore he opined that either of these would stand as a definition of algorithm. A reader first confronting the words that follow may well be confused, so a brief explanation is in order. *Calculation* means done by hand, *computation* means done by Turing machine (or equivalent). (Sometimes an author slips and interchanges the words). A "function" can be thought of as an "input-output box" into which a person puts natural numbers called "arguments" or "parameters" (but only the counting numbers including 0—the positive integers) and gets out a single positive integer (including 0) (conventionally called "the answer"). Think of the "function-box" as a little man either calculating by hand using "general recursion" or computing by Turing machine (or an equivalent machine). "Effectively calculable/computable" is more generic and means "calculable/computable by *some* procedure, method, technique ... whatever...". "General recursive" was Kleene's way of writing what today is called just "recursion"; however, "primitive recursion" — calculation by use of the five recursive operators—is a lesser form of recursion that lacks access to the sixth, additional, mu-operator that is needed only in rare instances. Thus most of life goes on requiring only the "primitive recursive functions."

1943 "Thesis I", 1952 "Church's Thesis"

In 1943 Kleene proposed what has come to be known as Church's thesis:

> "*Thesis I.* Every effectively calculable function (effectively decidable predicate) is general recursive" (First stated by Kleene in 1943 (reprinted page 274 in Davis, ed. *The Undecidable*; appears also verbatim in Kleene (1952) p.300)

In a nutshell: to calculate *any* function the only operations a person needs (technically, formally) are the 6 primitive operators of "general" recursion (nowadays called the operators of the mu recursive functions). Kleene's first statement of this was under the section title "12. Algorithmic theories". He would later amplify it in his text (1952) as follows:

> "Thesis I and its converse provide the exact definition of the notion of a calculation (decision) procedure or algorithm, for the case of a function (predicate) of natural numbers" (p. 301, boldface added for emphasis)

(His use of the word "decision" and "predicate" extends the notion of calculability to the more general manipulation of symbols such as occurs in mathematical "proofs".) This is not as daunting as it may sound — "general" recursion is just a way of making our everyday arithmetic operations from the five "operators" of the primitive recursive functions together with the additional mu-operator as needed. Indeed, Kleene gives 13 examples of primitive recursive functions and Boolos-Burgess-Jeffrey add some more, most of which will be familiar to the reader—e.g. addition, subtraction, multiplication and division, exponentiation, the CASE function, concatenation, etc, etc; for a list see Some common primitive recursive functions. Why general-recursive functions rather than primitive-recursive functions?

Kleene et al. (cf §55 General recursive functions p. 270 in Kleene 1952) had to add a sixth recursion operator called the minimization-operator (written as ì-operator or mu-operator) because Ackermann (1925) produced a hugely-growing function—the Ackermann function — and Rózsa Péter (1935) produced a general method of creating recursive functions using Cantor's diagonal argument, neither of which could be described by the 5 primitive-recursive-function operators. With respect to the Ackermann function:

> "...in a certain sense, the length of the computation [*sic*] algorithm of a recursive function which is not also primitive recursive grows faster with the arguments than the value of any primitive recursive function" (Kleene (1935) reprinted p. 246 in *The Undecidable*, plus footnote 13 with regards to the need for an additional operator, boldface added).

But the need for the mu-operator is a rarity. As indicated above by Kleene's list of common calculations, a person goes about their life happily computing primitive recursive functions without fear of encountering the monster numbers created by Ackermann's function (e.g. super-exponentiation).

1952 "Turing's Thesis"

Turing's Thesis hypothesizes the computability of "all computable functions" by the Turing machine model and its equivalents. To do this in an effective manner, Kleene extended the notion of "computable" by casting the net wider—by allowing into the notion of "functions" both "total functions" and "partial functions". A *total function* is one that is defined *for all natural numbers* (positive integers including 0). A partial function is defined for *some* natural numbers but not all—the specification of "some" has to come "up front". Thus the inclusion of "partial function" extends the notion of function to "less-perfect" functions. Total- and partial-functions may either be calculated by hand or computed by machine.

Examples:

"Functions": include "common subtraction m-n" and "addition m+n" "Partial function": "Common subtraction" m-n is undefined when only natural numbers (positive integers and zero) are allowed as input — e.g. 6-7 is undefined Total function: "Addition" m+n is defined for all positive integers and zero. We now observe Kleene's definition of "computable" in a formal sense: Definition: "A partial function ö is *computable*, if there is a machine

M which computes it" (Kleene (1952) p. 360) "Definition 2.5. An n-ary function $f(x_1,\ldots x_n)$ is partially computable if there exists a Turing machine Z such that

$$f(x_1,\ldots x_n) = \varnothing_Z^{(n)}(x_1,\ldots x_n)$$

In this case we say that [machine] Z computes f. If, in addition, $f(x_1,\ldots x_n)$ is a total function, then it is called computable" (Davis (1958) p. 10). Thus we have arrived at *Turing's Thesis*:

> "Every function which would naturally be regarded as computable is computable ... by one of his machines..." (Kleene (1952) p.376)

Although Kleene did not give examples of "computable functions" others have. For example, Davis (1958) gives Turing tables for the Constant, Successor and Identity functions, three of the five operators of the primitive recursive functions: Computable by Turing machine:

Addition (also is the Constant function if one operand is 0)

Increment (Successor function)

Common subtraction (defined only if x e" y). Thus "x - y" is an example of a partially computable function. Proper subtraction x4%y (as defined above) The identity function: for each i, a function $U_Z^n = \varnothing_Z^n(x_1,\ldots x_n)$ exists that plucks x_i out of the set of arguments $(x_1,\ldots x_n)$

Multiplication

Boolos-Burgess-Jeffrey (2002) give the following as prose descriptions of Turing machines for:

Doubling: 2*p

Parity

Addition

Multiplication

With regards to the counter machine, an abstract machine model equivalent to the Turing machine:

> Examples Computable by Abacus machine (cf Boolos-Burgess-Jeffrey (2002))
>
> Addition
>
> Multiplication
>
> Exponention: (a flow-chart/block diagram description of the algorithm)

Demonstrations of computability by abacus machine (Boolos-Burgess-Jeffrey (2002)) and by counter machine (Minsky 1967): The six recursive function operators:

1. Zero function
2. Successor function
3. Identity function
4. Composition function
5. Primitive recursion (induction)
6. Minimization

The fact that the abacus/counter machine models can simulate the recursive functions provides the proof that: If a function is "machine computable" then it is "hand-calculable by partial recursion". Kleene's Theorem XXIX :

> *"Theorem XXIX: "Every computable partial function ö is partial recursive..."* (italics in original, p. 374).

The converse appears as his Theorem XXVIII. Together these form the proof of their equivalence, Kleene's Theorem XXX.

1952 Church-Turing Thesis

With his Theorem XXX Kleene proves the *equivalence* of the two "Theses" — the Church Thesis and the Turing Thesis. (Kleene can only hypothesize (conjecture) the truth of both thesis — *these he has not proven*):

> *THEOREM XXX: The following classes of partial functions ... have the same members: (a) the partial recursive functions, (b) the computable functions ...*"(p. 376)
>
> Definition of "partial recursive function": "A partial function ö is partial recursive in [the partial functions] $ø_1$, ... $ø_n$ if there is a system of equations E which defines ö recursively from [partial functions] $ø_1$, ... $ø_n$" (p. 326)

Thus by Kleene's Theorem XXX: either method of making numbers from input-numbers—recursive functions calculated by hand or computated by Turing-machine or equivalent—results in an "*effectively calculable / computable* function".

If we accept the hypothesis that *every* calculation/ computation can be done by either method equivalently we have accepted both Kleene's Theorem XXX (the equivalence) and the Church-Turing Thesis (the hypothesis of "every").

A Bote of Dissent: "There's More to Algorithm..." Blass and Gurevich (2003)

The notion of separating out Church's and Turing's theses from the "Church-Turing thesis" appears not only in Kleene (1952) but in Blass-Gurevich (2003) as well. But there while there are agreements, there are disagreements too:

> "...we disagree with Kleene that the notion of algorithm is that well understood. In fact the notion of algorithm is richer these days than it was in Turing's days. And there are algorithms, of modern and classical varieties, not covered directly by Turing's analysis, for example, algorithms that interact with their environments, algorithms whose inputs are abstract structures, and geometric or, more generally, non-discrete algorithms" (Blass-Gurevich (2003) p. 8, boldface added)

1954 A.A. Markov's Characterization

A. A. Markov (1954) provided the following definition of algorithm:

> "1. In mathematics, "algorithm" is commonly understood to be an exact prescription, defining a computational process, leading from various initial data to the desired result...."

"The following three features are characteristic of algorithms and determine their role in mathematics:

"a) the precision of the prescription, leaving no place to arbitrariness, and its universal comprehensibility — the definiteness of the algorithm;

"b) the possibility of starting out with initial data, which may vary within given limits — the generality of the algorithm;

"c) the orientation of the algorithm toward obtaining some desired result, which is indeed obtained in the end with proper initial data — the conclusiveness of the algorithm." (p.1)

He admitted that this definition "does not pretend to mathematical precision" (p. 1). His 1954 monograph was his attempt to define algorithm more accurately; he saw his resulting definition—his "normal" algorithm—as "equivalent to the concept of a recursive function" (p. 3). His definition included four major components (Chapter II.3 pp. 63ff):

"1. Separate elementary steps, each of which will be performed according to one of [the substitution] rules... [rules given at the outset]

"2. ... steps of local nature ... [Thus the algorithm won't change more than a certain number of symbols to the left or right of the observed word/ symbol]

"3. Rules for the substitution formulas ... [he called the list of these "the scheme" of the algorithm]

"4. ...a means to distinguish a "concluding substitution" [i.e. a distinguishable "terminal/final" state or states]

In his Introduction Markov observed that "the entire significance for mathematics" of efforts to define algorithm more precisely would be "in connection with the problem of a constructive foundation for mathematics" (p. 2). Ian Stewart (cf Encyclopedia Britannica) shares a similar belief: "...constructive analysis is very much in the same algorithmic spirit as computer science...". For more see constructive mathematics and Intuitionism. Distinguishability and Locality: Both notions first appeared with Turing (1936–1937) —

> "The new observed squares must be immediately recognizable by the computer [*sic*: a computer was a person in 1936]. I think it reasonable to suppose that they can only be squares whose distance from the closest of the immediately observed squares does not exceed a certain fixed amount. Let us stay that each of the new observed squares is within L squares of one of the previously observed squares." (Turing (1936) p. 136 in Davis ed. *Undecidable*)

Locality appears prominently in the work of Gurevich and Gandy (1980) (whom Gurevich cites). Gandy's "Fourth Principle for Mechanisms" is "The Principle of Local Causality":

> "We now come to the most important of our principles. In Turing's analysis the requirement that the action depend only on a bounded portion of the record was based on a human limitiation. We replace this by a physical limitation which we call the *principle of local causation.* Its justification lies in the finite velocity of propagation of effects and signals: contemporary physics rejects the possibility of

instantaneous action at a distance." (Gandy (1980) p. 135 in J. Barwise et al.)

1936, 1963, 1964 Godel's Characterization

1936: A rather famous quote from Kurt Gödel appears in a "Remark added in proof [of the original German publication] in his paper "On the Length of Proofs" translated by Martin Davis appearing on pp. 82–83 of *The Undecidable*. A number of authors—Kleene, Gurevich, Gandy etc. — have quoted the following:

> "Thus, the concept of "computable" is in a certain definite sense "absolute," while practically all other familiar metamathematical concepts (e.g. provable, definable, etc.) depend quite essentially on the system with respect to which they are defined." (p. 83)

1963: In a "Note" dated 28 August 1963 added to his famous paper *On Formally Undecidable Propostions* (1931) Gödel states (in a footnote) his belief that "formal systems" have "the characteristic property that reasoning in them, in principle, can be completely replaced by mechanical devices" (p. 616 in van Heijenoort). ". . . due to "A. M. Turing's work a precise and unquestionaly adequate definition of the general notion of formal system can now be given [and] a completely general version of Theorems VI and XI is now possible." (p. 616). In a 1964 note to another work he expresses the same opinion more strongly and in more detail.

1964: In a Postscriptum, dated 1964, to a paper presented to the Institute for Advanced Study in spring 1934, Gödel amplified his conviction that "formal systems" are those that can be mechanized:

> "In consequence of later advances, in particular of the fact that, due to A. M. Turing's work, a precise and unquestionably adequate definition of the general concept of formal system can now be given . . . Turing's work gives an analysis of the concept of

> "mechanical procedure" (alias "algorithm" or "computational procedure" or "finite combinatorial procedure"). This concept is shown to be equivalent with that of a "Turing machine".* A formal system can simply be defined to be any mechanical procedure for producing formulas, called provable formulas . . . ." (p. 72 in Martin Davis ed. *The Undecidable*: "Postscriptum" to "On Undecidable Propositions of Formal Mathematical Systems" appearing on p. 39, loc. cit.)

The * indicates a footnote in which Gödel cites the papers by Allan Turing (1937) and Emil Post (1936) and then goes on to make the following intriguing statement:

> "As for previous equivalent definitions of computability, which however, are much less suitable for our purpose, see Alonzo Church, Am. J. Math., vol. 58 (1936) [appearing in *The Undecidable* pp. 100-102]).

Church's definitions encompass so-called "recursion" and the "lambda calculus" (i.e. the ë-definable functions). His footnote 18 says that he discussed the relationship of "effective calculatibility" and "recursiveness" with Gödel but that he independently questioned "effectively calculability" and "ë-definability":

> "We now define the notion . . . of an effectively calculable function of positive integers by identifying it with the notion of a recursive function of positive integers[18] (or of a ë-definable function of positive integers.
>
> "It has already been pointed out that, for every function of positive integers which is effectively calculable in the sense just defined, there exists an algorithm for the calculation of its value.
>
> "Conversely it is true . . ." (p. 100, The Undecidable).

It would appear from this, and the following, that far

as Gödel was concerned, the Turing machine was sufficient and the lambda calculus was "much less suitable."

He goes on to make the point that, with regards to limitations on human reason, the jury is still out:

> ("Note that the question of whether there exist finite non-mechanical procedures not equivalent with any algorithm, has nothing whatsoever to do with the adequacy of the definition of "formal system" and of "mechanical procedure.") (p. 72, loc. cit.)
>
> "(For theories and procedures in the more general sense indicated in footnote the situation may be different. Note that the results mentioned in the postcript do not establish any bounds for the powers of human reason, but rather for the potentialities of pure formalism in mathematics.) (p. 73 loc. cit.)

1967 Minsky's Characterization

Minsky (1967) baldly asserts that "an algorithm is "an effective procedure" and declines to use the word "algorithm" further in his text; in fact his index makes it clear what he feels about "Algorithm, *synonym* for Effective procedure"(p. 311):

> "We will use the latter term [an *effective procedure*] in the sequel. The terms are roughly synonymous, but there are a number of shades of meaning used in different contexts, especially for 'algorithm'" (italics in original, p. 105)

Other writers use the word "effective procedure".

This leads one to wonder: What is Minsky's notion of "an effective procedure"? He starts off with:

> "...a set of rules which tell us, from moment to moment, precisely how to behave" (p. 106)

But he recognizes that this is subject to a criticism:

> "... the criticism that the interpretation of the rules is left to depend on some person or agent" (p. 106)

His refinement? To "specify, along with the statement of the rules, *the details of the mechanism that is to interpret them*". To avoid the "cumbersome" process of "having to do this over again for each individual procedure" he hopes to identify a "reasonably *uniform* family of rule-obeying mechanisms". His "formulation":

> "(1) a *language* in which sets of behavioural rules are to be expressed, and "(2) a *single* machine which can interpret statements in the language and thus carry out the steps of each specified process." (italics in original, all quotes this para. p. 107)

In the end, though, he still worries that "there remains a subjective aspect to the matter. Different people may not agree on whether a certain procedure should be called effective" (p. 107). But Minsky is undeterred. He immediately introduces "Turing's Analysis of Computation Process" (his chapter 5.2). He quotes what he calls "Turing's *thesis*"

> "Any process which could naturally be called an effective procedure can be realized by a Turing machine" (p. 108. (Minsky comments that in a more general form this is called "*Church's thesis*").

After an analysis of "Turing's Argument" (his chapter 5.3) he observes that "equivalence of many intuitive formulations" of Turing, Church, Kleene, Post, and Smullyan "...leads us to suppose that there is really here an 'objective' or 'absolute' notion. As Rogers [1959] put it:

> "In this sense, the notion of effectively computable function is one of the few 'absolute' concepts produced by modern work in the foundations of mathematics'" (Minsky p. 111 quoting Rogers, Hartley Jr (1959) *The present theory of Turing machine computability*, J. SIAM 7, 114-130.)

1967 Rogers' Characterization

In his 1967 *Theory of Recursive Functions and Effective Computability* Hartley Rogers' characterizes "algorithm" roughly as "a clerical (i.e., deterministic, bookkeeping) procedure . . . applied to . . . symbolic *inputs* and which will eventually yield, for each such input, a corresponding symbolic *output*"(p. 1). He then goes on to describe the notion "in approximate and intuitive terms" as having 10 "features", 5 of which he asserts that "virtually all mathematicians would agree [to]" (p. 2). The remaining 5 he asserts "are less obvious than *1 to *5 and about which we might find less general agreement" (p. 3). The 5 "obvious" are:

- 1 An algorithm is a set of instructions of finite size,
- 2 There is a capable computing agent,
- 3 "There are facilities for making, storing, and retrieving steps in a computation"
- 4 Given #1 and #2 the agent computes in "discrete stepwise fashion" without use of continuous methods or analogue devices",
- 5 The computing agent carries the computation forward "without resort to random methods or devices, e.g., dice" (in a footnote Rogers wonders if #4 and #5 are really the same)

The remaining 5 that he opens to debate, are:

- 6 No fixed bound on the size of the inputs,
- 7 No fixed bound on the size of the set of instructions,
- 8 No fixed bound on the amount of memory storage available,
- 9 A fixed finite bound on the capacity or ability of the computing agent (Rogers illustrates with

example simple mechanisms similar to a Post-Turing machine or a counter machine),

- 10 A bound on the length of the computation — "should we have some idea, 'ahead of time', how long the computationwill take?" (p. 5). Rogers requires "only that a computation terminate after *some* finite number of steps; we do not insist on an a priori ability to estimate this number." (p. 5).

1968, 1973 Knuth's Characterization

Knuth (1968, 1973) has given a list of five properties that are widely accepted as requirements for an algorithm:

1. Finiteness: "An algorithm must always terminate after a finite number of steps ... a *very* finite number, a reasonable number"
2. Definiteness: "Each step of an algorithm must be precisely defined; the actions to be carried out must be rigorously and unambiguously specified for each case"
3. Input: "...quantities which are given to it initially before the algorithm begins. These inputs are taken from specified sets of objects"
4. Output: "...quantities which have a specified relation to the inputs"
5. Effectiveness: "... all of the operations to be performed in the algorithm must be sufficiently basic that they can in principle be done exactly and in a finite length of time by a man using paper and pencil"

Knuth offers as an example the Euclidean algorithm for determining the greatest common divisor of two natural numbers (cf. Knuth Vol. 1 p. 2). Knuth admits that, while his description of an algorithm may be intuitively clear, it lacks formal rigor, since it is not exactly clear what "precisely defined" means, or "rigorously and unambiguously specified" means, or "sufficiently basic", and so forth. He makes an effort in this direction in his first volume where he defines *in detail* what he calls the "machine language" for his "mythical MIX...the world's first polyunsaturated computer" (pp. 120ff). Many of the algorithms in his books are written in the MIX language. He also uses tree diagrams, flow diagrams and state diagrams.

> "Goodness" of an algorithm, "best" algorithms: Knuth states that "In practice, we not only want algorithms, we want *good* algorithms...." He suggests that some criteria of an algorithm's goodness are the number of steps to perform the algorithm, its "adaptability to computers, its simplicity and elegance, etc." Given a number of algorithms to perform the same computation, which one is "best"? He calls this sort of inquiry "algorithmic analysis: given an algorithm, to determine its performance characteristcis" (all quotes this paragraph: Knuth Vol. 1 p. 7)

1972 Stone's Characterization

Stone (1972) and Knuth (1968, 1973) were professors at Stanford University at the same time so it is not surprising if there are similarities in their definitions (boldface added for emphasis):

> "To summarize ... we define an algorithm to be a set of rules that precisely defines a sequence of operations such that each rule is effective and definite and such that the sequence terminates in a finite time." (boldface added, p. 8)

Stone is noteworthy because of his detailed discussion of what constitutes an "effective" rule – his robot, or person-acting-as-robot, must have some information and abilities within them, and if not the information and the ability must be provided in "the algorithm":

> "For people to follow the rules of an algorithm, the

> rules must be formulated so that they can be followed in a robot-like manner, that is, without the need for thought... however, if the instructions [to solve the quadratic equation, his example] are to be obeyed by someone who knows how to perform arithmetic operations but does not know how to extract a square root, then we must also provide a set of rules for extracting a square root in order to satisfy the definition of algorithm" (p. 4-5)

Furthermore "...not all instructions are acceptable, because they may require the robot to have abilities beyond those that we consider reasonable." He gives the example of a robot confronted with the question is "Henry VIII a King of England?" and to print 1 if yes and 0 if no, but the robot has not been previously provided with this information. And worse, if the robot is asked if Aristotle was a King of England and the robot only had been provided with five names, it would not know how to answer. Thus:

> "an intuitive definition of an acceptable sequence of instructions is one in which each instruction is precisely defined so that the robot is guaranteed to be able to obey it" (p. 6)

After providing us with his definition, Stone introduces the Turing machine model and states that the set of five-tuples that are the machine's instructions are "an algorithm ... known as a Turing machine program" (p. 9). Immediately thereafter he goes on say that a "*computation* of a Turing machine is *described* by stating:

"1. The tape alphabet

"2. The form in which the [input] parameters are presented on the tape

"3. The initial state of the Turing machine

"4. The form in which answers [output] will be represented on the tape when the Turing machine halts

"5. The machine programme" (italics added, p. 10)

This precise prescription of what is required for "a computation" is in the spirit of what will follow in the work of Blass and Gurevich.

1995 Soare's Characterization

"A *computation* is a process whereby we proceed from initially given objects, called *inputs*, according to a fixed set of rules, called a *programme, procedure,* or *algorithm*, through a series of *steps* and arrive at the end of these steps with a final result, called the *output*. The algorithm, as a set of rules proceeding from inputs to output, must be precise and definite with each successive step clearly determined. The concept of *computability* concerns those objects which may be specified in principle by computations . . ."

2000 Berlinski's Characterization

While a student at Princeton in the mid-1960s, David Berlinski was a student of Alonzo Church (cf p. 160). His year-2000 book *The Advent of the Algorithm: The 300-year Journey from an Idea to the Computer* contains the following definition of algorithm:

> *"In the logician's voice:*
> *"an algorithm is*
> *a finite procedure,*
> *written in a fixed symbolic vocabulary,*
> *governed by precise instructions,*
> *moving in discrete steps, 1, 2, 3, . . .,*
> *whose execution requires no insight, cleverness,*
> *intuition, intelligence, or perspicuity,*
> *and that sooner or later comes to an end."'* (boldface and italics in the original, p. xviii)

2000, 2002 Gurevich's Characterization

A careful reading of Gurevich 2000 leads one to conclude

(infer?) that he believes that "an algorithm" is actually "a Turing machine" or "a pointer machine" doing a computation. An "algorithm" is not just the symbol-table that guides the behaviour of the machine, nor is it just one instance of a machine doing a computation given a particular set of input parameters, nor is it a suitably-programmed machine with the power off; rather *an algorithm is the machine actually doing any computation of which it is capable.* Gurevich does not come right out and say this, so as worded above this conclusion (inference?) is certainly open to debate:

> " . . . every algorithm can be simulated by a Turing machine . . . a programme can be simulated and therefore given a precise meaning by a Turing machine." (p. 1)

> " It is often thought that the problem of formalizing the notion of sequential algorithm was solved by Church [1936] and Turing [1936]. For example, according to Savage [1987], an algorithm is a computational *process* defined by a Turing machine. Church and Turing did not solve the problem of formalizing the notion of sequential algorithm. Instead they gave (different but equivalent) formalizations of the notion of computable function, and there is more to an algorithm than the function it computes. (italics added p. 3)

> "Of course, the notions of algorithm and computable function are intimately related: by definition, a computable function is a function computable by an algorithm. . . . (p. 4)

In Blass and Gurevich 2002 the authors invoke a dialog between "Quisani" ("Q") and "Authors" (A), using Yiannis Moshovakis as a foil, where they come right out and flatly state:

> "A: To localize the disagreement, let's first mention two points of agreement. First, there are some things

> that are obviously algorithms by anyone's definition — Turing machines, sequential-time ASMs [Abstract State Machines], and the like. . . .Second, at the other extreme are specifications that would not be regarded as algorithms under anyone's definition, since they give no indication of how to compute anything . . . The issue is how detailed the information has to be in order to count as an algorithm. . . . Moshovakis allows some things that we would call only declarative specifications, and he would probably use the word "implementation" for things that we call algorithms." (paragraphs joined for ease of readability, 2002:22)

This use of the word "implementation" cuts straight to the heart of the question. Early in the paper, Q states his reading of Moshovakis:

> "...[H]e would probably think that your practical work [Gurevich works for Microsoft] forces you to think of implementations more than of algorithms. He is quite willing to identify implementations with machines, but he says that algorithms are something more general. What it boils down to is that you say an algorithm is a machine and Moschovakis says it is not." (2002:3)

But the authors waffle here, saying "[L]et's stick to "algorithm" and "machine", and the reader is left, again, confused. We have to wait until Dershowitz and Gurevich 2007 to get the following footnote comment:

> " . . . Nevertheless, if one accepts Moshovakis's point of view, then it is the "implementation" of algorithms that we have set out to characterize."(cf Footnote 9 2007:6)

2003 Blass and Gurevich's Characterization

Blass and Gurevich describe their work as evolved from consideration of Turing machines and pointer machines, specifically Kolmogorov-Uspensky machines (KU machines),

Schönhage Storage Modification Machines (SMM), and linking automata as defined by Knuth. The work of Gandy and Markov are also described as influential precursors. Gurevich offers a 'strong' definition of an algorithm (boldface added):

> "...Turing's informal argument in favour of his thesis justifies a stronger thesis: every algorithm can be simulated by a Turing machine....In practice, it would be ridiculous...[Nevertheless,] [c]an one generalize Turing machines so that any algorithm, never mind how abstract, can be modeled by a generalized machine?...But suppose such generalized Turing machines exist. What would their states be?...a first-order structure ... a particular small instruction set suffices in all cases ... computation as an evolution of the state ... could be nondeterministic... can interact with their environment ... [could be] parallel and multi-agent ... [could have] dynamic semantics ... [the two underpinings of their work are:] Turing's thesis ...[and] the notion of (first order) structure of [Tarski 1933]" (Gurevich 2000, p. 1-2)

The above phrase computation as an evolution of the state differs markedly from the definition of Knuth and Stone—the "algorithm" as a Turing machine programme. Rather, it corresponds to what Turing called *the complete configuration* (cf Turing's definition in Undecidable, p. 118) — and includes *both* the current instruction (state) *and* the status of the tape. [cf Kleene (1952) p. 375 where he shows an example of a tape with 6 symbols on it—all other squares are blank—and how to Gödelize its combined table-tape status]. In Algorithm examples we see the evolution of the state first-hand.

1995 – Daniel Dennett: Evolution as an Algorithmic Process

Philosopher Daniel Dennett analyses the importance of evolution as an algorithmic process in his 1995 book

Darwin's Dangerous Idea. Dennett identifies three key features of an algorithm:

- Substrate neutrality: an algorithm relies on its *logical* structure. Thus, the particular form in which an algorithm is manifested is not important (Dennett's example is long division: it works equally well on paper, on parchment, on a computer screen, or using neon lights or in skywriting). (p. 51)
- Underlying mindlessness: no matter how complicated the end-product of the algorithmic process may be, each step in the algorithm is sufficiently simple to be performed by a non-sentient, mechanical device. The algorithm does not require a "brain" to maintain or operate it. "The standard textbook analogy notes that algorithms are *recipes* of sorts, designed to be followed by *novice* cooks."(p. 51)
- Guaranteed results: If the algorithm is executed correctly, it will always produce the same results. "An algorithm is a foolproof recipe."(p. 51)

It is on the basis of this analysis that Dennett concludes that "According to Darwin, evolution is an algorithmic process" (p. 60). However, in the previous page he has gone out on a much-further limb. In the context of his chapter titled "Processes as Algorithms" he states:

> "But then . . are there any limits at all on what may be considered an algorithmic process? I guess the answer is NO; if you wanted to, you can treat any process at the abstract level as an algorithmic process. . . If what strikes you as puzzling is the uniformity of the [ocean's] sand grains or the strength of the [tempered-steel] blade, an algorithmic explanation is what will satisfy your curiosity — and it will be the truth. . . .
>
> "No matter how impressive the products of an

> algorithm, the underlying process always consists of nothing but a set of individualy [*sic*] mindless steps succeeding each other without the help of any intelligent supervision; they are 'automatic' by definition: the workings of an automaton." (p. 59)

It is unclear from the above whether Dennett is stating that the physical world by itself and without observers is intrinsically algorithmic (computational) or whether a symbol-processing observer is what is adding "meaning" to the observations.

2002 John Searle Adds a Clarifying Caveat to Dennett's Characterization

John R. Searle and Daniel Dennett having been poking at one-another's philosophies of mind (cf philosophy of mind) for the past 30 years. Dennett hews to the Strong AI point of view that the logical structure of an algorithm is sufficient to explain mind; Searle, of Chinese room fame claims that logical structure is not sufficient, rather that: "Syntax [i.e. logical structure] is by itself not sufficient for semantic content [i.e. meaning]" (italics in original, Searle 2002:16). In other words, the "meaning" of symbols is relative to the mind that is using them; an algorithm—a logical construct—by itself is insufficient for a mind. Searle urges a note of caution to those who want to define algorithmic (computational) processes as intrinsic to nature (e.g. cosmology, physics, chemistry, etc.):

> "Computation . . . is observer-relative, and this is because computation is defined in terms of symbol manipulation, but the notion of a 'symbol' is not a notion of physics or chemistry. Something is a symbol only if it is used, treated or regarded as a symbol. The chinese room argument showed that semantics is not intrinsic to syntax. But what this shows is that syntax is not intrinsic to physics. . . . Something is a symbol only relative to some observer, user or agent who assigns a symbolic interpretation to it. .

> . you can assign a computational interpretation to anything. But if the question asks, 'Is consciousness intrinsically computational?' the answer is: *nothing is intrinsically computational*. Computation exists only relative to some agent or observer who imposes a computational interpretation on some phenomenon. This is an obvious point. I should have seen it ten years ago but I did not." (italics added, p. 17)

2002: Boolos-Burgess-Jeffrey Specification of Turing Machine Calculation

An example in Boolos-Burgess-Jeffrey (2002) (pp. 31–32) demonstrates the precision required in a complete specification of an algorithm, in this case to add two numbers: m+n. It is similar to the Stone requirements above.

(i) They have discussed the role of "number format" in the computation and selected the "tally notation" to represent numbers:

> "Certainly computation can be harder in practice with some notations than others... But... it is possible in principle to do in any other notation, simply by translating the data... For purposes of framing a rigorously defined notion of computability, it is convenient to use monadic or tally notation" (p. 25-26)

(ii) At the outset of their example they specify the machine to be used in the computation as a Turing machine. They have previously specified (p. 26) that the Turing-machine will be of the 4-tuple, rather than 5-tuple, variety. For more on this convention see Turing machine.

(iii) Previously the authors have specified that the tape-head's position will be indicated by a subscript to the *right* of the scanned symbol. For more on this convention see Turing machine. (In the following, boldface is added for emphasis):

"We have not given an official definition of what it is for a numerical function to be computable by a Turing machine, specifying how inputs or arguments are to be represented on the machine, and how outputs or values represented. Our specifications for a k-place function from positive integers to positive integers are as follows:

"(a) [Initial number format:] The arguments m_1, ... m_k, ... will be represented in monadic [unary] notation by blocks of those numbers of strokes, each block separated from the next by a single blank, on an otherwise blank tape.
Example: 3+2, 111B11

"(b) [Initial head location, initial state:] Initially, the machine will be scanning the leftmost 1 on the tape, and will be in its initial state, state 1.
Example: 3+2, $1_1$111B11

"(c) [Successful computation — number format at Halt:] If the function to be computed assigns a value n to the arguments that are represented initially on the tape, then the machine will eventually halt on a tape containing a block of strokes, and otherwise blank...
Example: 3+2, 11111

"(d) [Successful computation — head location at Halt:] In this case [c] the machine will halt scanning the left-most 1 on the tape...
Example: 3+2, 1_n1111

"(e) [Unsuccessful computation — failure to Halt or Halt with non-standard number format:] If the function that is to be computed assigns no value to the arguments that are represented initially on the tape, then the machine either will never halt, or will halt in some nonstandard configuration..."(ibid)
Example: B_n11111 or $B11_n$111 or $B11111_n$

This specification is incomplete: it requires the location of where the instructions are to be placed and their format in the machine—

(iv) in the finite state machine's TABLE or, in the case of a Universal Turing machine on the tape, and

(v) the Table of instructions in a specified format.

This later point is important. Boolos-Burgess-Jeffrey give a demonstration (p. 36) that the predictability of the entries in the table allow one to "shrink" the table by putting the entries in sequence and omitting the input state and the symbol.

2006: Sipser's Assertion and His Three Levels of Description

For examples of this specification-method applied to the addition algorithm "m+n" see Algorithm examples. Sipser begins by defining '"algorithm" as follows:

> "Informally speaking, an *algorithm* is a collection of simple instructions for carrying out some task. Commonplace in everyday life, algorithms sometimes are called *procedures* or *recipes* (italics in original, p. 154)
>
> "...our real focus from now on is on algorithms. That is, the Turing machine merely serves as a precise model for the definition of algorithm .... we need only to be comfortable enough with Turing machines to believe that they capture all algorithms" (p. 156)

Does Sipser mean that "algorithm" is just "instructions" for a Turing machine, or is the combination of "instructions + a (specific variety of) Turing machine"? For example, he defines the two standard variants (multi-tape and non-deterministic) of his particular variant (not the same as Turing's original) and goes on, in his Problems (pages 160-

161), to describes four more variants (write-once, doubly-infinite tape (i.e. left- and right-infinite), left reset, and "stay put instead of left). In addition, he imposes some constraints. First, the input must be encoded as a string (p. 157) and says of numeric encodings in the context of complexity theory:

> "But note that unary notation for encoding numbers (as in the number 17 encoded by the uary string 11111111111111111) isn't reasonable because it is exponentially larger than truly reasonable encodings, such as base *k* notation for any *k* e" 2."(p. 259)

van Emde Boas comments on a similar problem with respect to the random access machine (RAM) abstract model of computation sometimes used in place of the Turing machine when doing "analysis of algorithms": "The absence or presence of multiplicative and parallel bit manipulation operations is of relevance for the correct understanding of some results in the analysis of algorithms.

> ". . . [T]here hardly exists such as a thing as an "innocent" extension of the standard RAM model in the uniform time measures; either one only has additive arithmetic or one might as well include all reasonable multiplicative and/or bitwise Boolean instructions on small operands." (van Emde Boas, 1990:26)

With regards to a "description language" for algorithms Sipser finishes the job that Stone and Boolos-Burgess-Jeffrey started (boldface added). He offers us three levels of description of Turing machine algorithms (p. 157): High-level description: "wherein we use ... prose to describe an algorithm, ignoring the implementation details. At this level we do not need to mention how the machine manages its tape or head." Implementation description: "in which we use ... prose to describe the way that the Turing machine moves its head and the way that it stores data on its tape. At this level we do not give details of states or transition function." Formal description: "... the lowest, most detailed, level of description... that spells out in full the Turing machine's states, transition function, and so on."

ALGORITHM EXAMPLES

An Example: Algorithm Specification of Addition m+n

Choice of machine model: There is no "best", or "preferred" model. The Turing machine, while considered the standard, is notoriously awkward to use. And different problems seem to require different models to study them. Many researchers have observed these problems, for example:

> "The principal purpose of this paper is to offer a theory which is closely related to Turing's but is more economical in the basic operations" (Wang (1954) p. 63)

"Certain features of Turing machines have induced later workers to propose alternative devices as embodiments of what is to be meant by effective computability.... a Turing machine has a certain opacity, its workings are known rather than seen. Further a Turing machine is inflexible ... a Turing machine is slow in (hypothetical) operation and, usually complicated. This makes it rather hard to design it, and even harder to investigate such matters as time or storage optimization or a comparison between efficiency of two algorithms." (Melzak (1961) p. 281) Shepherdson-Sturgis (1963) proposed their register-machine model because "these proofs [using Turing machines] are complicated and tedious to follow for two reasons: (1) A Turing machine has only one head... (2) It has only one tape...." They were in search of "a form of idealized computer which is sufficiently flexible for one to be able to convert an intuitive computational procedure into a programme for such a machine" (p. 218).

> "I would prefer something along the lines of the random access computers of Angluin and Valiant [as opposed to the pointer machine of Schönhage]" (Gurivich 1988 p. 6)
>
> "Showing that a function is Turing computable directly...is rather laborious ... we introduce an ostensibly more flexible kind of idealized machine, an abacus machine..." (Boolos-Burgess-Jeffrey 2002 p.45).

About all that one can insist upon is that the algorithm-writer specify in exacting detail (i) the machine model to be used and (ii) its instruction set. Atomization of the instruction set:

> The Turing machine model is primitive, but not as primitive as it can be. As noted in the above quotes this is a source of concern when studying complexity and equivalence of algorithms. Although the observations quoted below concern the Random access machine model – a Turing-machine equivalent – the problem remains for any Turing-equivalent model:
>
> "...there hardly exists such a thing as an 'innocent' extension of the standard RAM model in the uniform time measure; either one only has additive arithmetic, or one might as well include all multiplicative and/ or bitwise Boolean instructions on small operands...." (van Emde Boas (1992) p. 26)
>
> "Since, however, the computational power of a RAM model seems to depend rather sensitively on the scope of its instruction set, we nevertheless will have to go into detail...
>
> "One important principle will be to admit only such instructions which can be said to be of an *atomistic* nature. We will describe two versions of the so-called *successor* RAM, with the successor function as the only arithmetic operation....the RAM0 version deserves special attention for its extreme simplicity;

> its instruction set consists of only a few one letter codes, without any (explicit) addressing." (Schönhage (1980) p.494)

Example #1: The most general (and original) Turing machine – single-tape with left-end, multi-symbols, 5-tuple instruction format – can be atomized into the Turing machine of Boolos-Burgess-Jeffrey (2002) – single-tape with no ends, two "symbols" { B, | } (where B symbolizes "blank square" and | symbolizes "marked square"), and a 4-tuple instruction format. This model in turn can be further atomized into a Post-Turing machine – single-tape with no ends, two symbols { B, | }, and a 0- and 1-parameter instruction set (e.g. { Left, Right, Mark, Erase, Jump-if-marked to instruction xxx, Jump-if-blank to instruction xxx, Halt }). Example #2: The RASP can be reduced to a RAM by moving its instructions off the tape and (perhaps with translation) into its finite-state machine "table" of instructions, the RAM stripped of its indirect instruction and reduced to a 2- and 3-operand "abacus" register machine; the abacus in turn can be reduced to the 1- and 2-operand Minsky (1967)/ Shepherdson-Sturgis (1963) counter machine, which can be further atomized into the 0- and 1-operand instructions of Schönhage (and even a 0-operand Schönhage-like instruction set is possible).

Cost of Atomization

Atomization comes at a (usually severe) cost: while the resulting instructions may be "simpler", atomization (usually) creates *more* instructions and the need for *more computational steps*. As shown in the following example the increase in computation steps may be significant (i.e. orders of magnitude – the following example is "tame"), and atomization may (but not always, as in the case of the Post-Turing model) reduce the usability and readability of "the machine code". For more see Turing tarpit.

REFERENCES

Andreas Blass and Yuri Gurevich (2003), *Algorithms: A Quest for Absolute Definitions*, Bulletin of European Association for Theoretical Computer Science 81, 2003. Includes an excellent bibliography of 56 references.

Burgin, M. *Super-recursive algorithms*, Monographs in computer science, Springer, 2005.

David Berlinski (2000), *The Advent of the Algorithm: The 300-Year Journey from an Idea to the Computer*, Harcourt, Inc., San Diego,

Davis, Martin (1958). *Computability & Unsolvability*. New York: McGraw-Hill Book Company, Inc.. . A source of important definitions and some Turing machine-based algorithms for a few recursive functions.

Davis, Martin (1965). *The Undecidable: Basic Papers On Undecidable Propostions, Unsolvable Problems and Computable Functions*. New York: Raven Press. Davis gives commentary before each article. Papers of Gödel, Alonzo Church, Turing, Rosser, Kleene, and Emil Post are included.

Dennett, Daniel (1995). *Darwin's Dangerous Idea*. New York: Touchstone/Simon & Schuster.

George Boolos, John P. Burgess, Richard Jeffrey (2002), *Computability and Logic: Fourth Edition*, Cambridge University Press, Cambridge, UK.

Kleene C., Stephen (1943). "Recursive Predicates and Quantifiers". *American Mathematical Society Transactions* (Transactions of the American Mathematical Society, Vol. 53, No. 1) 54 (1): 41–73.

Kleene, Stephen C. (First Edition 1952). *Introduction to Metamathematics* (Tenth Edition 1991 ed.). North-Holland Publishing Company. Excellent — accessible, readable — reference source for mathematical "foundations".

Knuth, Donald E.. (First Edition 1968). *The Art of Computer Programming Second Edition, Volumne 1/Fundamental Algorithms* (2nd, 1973 ed.). Addison-Wesley Publishing Company. The first of Knuth's famous series of three texts.

Lewis, H.R. and Papadimitriou, C.H. *Elements of the Theory of Computation*, Prentice-Hall, Uppre Saddle River, N.J., 1998

Robin Gandy, *Church's Thesis and principles for Mechanisms*, in J.Barwise, H.J. Keisler and K.Kunen, eds., *The Kleene*

Symposium, North-Holland Publishing Company 1980) pp. 123–148. Gandy's famous "4 principles of [computational] mechanisms" includes "Principle IV — The Principle of Local Causality".

Yuri Gurevich, *Sequential Abstract State Machines Capture Sequential Algorithms*, ACM Transactions on Computational Logic, Vol 1, no 1 (July 2000), pages 77–111. Includes bibliography of 33 sources.

2

Algorithm: Focus on Abstract Machine, Design and Engineering

ABSTRACT MACHINE

An abstract machine, also called an abstract computer, is a theoretical model of a computer hardware or software system used in automata theory. Abstraction of computing processes is used in both the computer science and computer engineering disciplines and usually assumes discrete time paradigm. In the theory of computation, abstract machines are often used in thought experiments regarding computability or to analyze the complexity of algorithms. A typical abstract machine consists of a definition in terms of input, output, and the set of allowable operations used to turn the former into the latter. The best-known example is the Turing machine. More complex definitions create abstract machines with full instruction sets, registers and models of memory. One popular model more similar to real modern machines is the RAM model, which allows random access to indexed memory locations. As the performance difference between different levels of cache memory grows, cache-sensitive models such as the external-memory model and cache-oblivious model are growing in importance.

An abstract machine can also refer to a microprocessor design which has yet to be (or is not intended to be) implemented as hardware. An abstract machine implemented as a software simulation, or for which an interpreter exists, is called a virtual machine. Through the use of abstract machines it is possible to compute the amount of resources (time, memory, etc.) necessary to perform a particular operation without having to construct an actual system to do it.

Articles Concerning Turing-Equivalent Sequential Abstract Machine Models

An approach is to take a somewhat formal taxonomic approach to classify the Turing equivalent abstract machines. This taxonomy does not include finite automata:

Family: Turing-equivalent (TE) abstract machine:

Subfamilies:

Subfamily (1) Sequential TE abstract machine

Subfamily (2) Parallel TE abstract machine

Subfamily (1)— *Sequential* TE abstract machine model: There are two classes (genera) of Sequential TE abstract machine models currently in use (cf van Emde Boas, for example):

Genus (1.1) Tape-based Turing machine model

Genus (1.2) Register-based register machine

Genus (1.1) — Tape-based Turing machine model: This includes the following "species":

{single tape, Multi-tape Turing machine, deterministic Turing machine, Non-deterministic Turing machine, Wang B-machine, Post-Turing machine, Oracle machine, Universal Turing machine }

Genus (1.2)— The register machine model: This includes (at least) the following four "species" (others are mentioned by van Emde Boas):

{(1.2.1) Counter machine, (1.2.2) Random access machine RAM, (1.2.3) Random access stored programme machine RASP, (1.2.4) Pointer machine}

Species (1.2.1) — Counter machine model:

{abacus machine, Lambek machine, Melzak model, Minsky machine, Shepherdson-Sturgis machine, programme machine, etc.}

Species (1.2.2) — Random access machine (RAM) model:

{any counter-machine model with additional *indirect addressing*, but with instructions in the state machine in the Harvard architecture; any model with an "accumulator" with additional indirect addressing but instructions in the state machine in the Harvard architecture}

Species (1.2.3) — Random access stored programme machine (RASP) model includes

{any RAM with programme stored in the registers similar to the Universal Turing machine i.e. in the von Neumann architecture}

Species (1.2.4)— Pointer machine model includes the following:

= { Schönhage Storage Modification Machine SMM, Kolmogorov-Uspensky KU-machine, Knuth linking automaton}

Other Abstract Machines

- ABC programming language
- Abstract Machine Notation
- ALF programming language
- Categorical Abstract Machine Language
- Context-free grammar
- Finite automata

- Specification and Design Language
- Historycal/Simplicity Abstract Machines for Prolog:
  - o 1.Vienna Abstract Machine (VAM Prolog)
  - o 2.Warren Abstract Machine (WAM Prolog)
  - o 3.Berkeley Abstract Machine (BAM Prolog).
- MMIX
- MikroSim
- Ten15
- TenDRA Distribution Format

ALGORITHM DESIGN

Algorithm design is a specific method to create a mathematical process in solving problems. Applied algorithm design is algorithm engineering. Algorithm design is identified and incorporated into many solution theories of operation research, such as dynamic programming and divide-and-conquer. Techniques for designing and implementing algorithm designs are algorithm design patterns, such as template method patterns and decorator patterns, and uses of data structures, and name and sort lists. Some current day uses of algorithm design can be found in internet retrieval processes of web crawling, packet routing and caching. Mainframe programming languages such as ALGOL (for *Algo*rithmic *l*anguage), FORTRAN, COBOL, PL/I, SAIL, and SNOBOL are computing tools to implement an "algorithm design"... but, an "algorithm design" (a/d) is not a language. An a/d can be a hand written process, eg. set of equations, a series of mechanical processes done by hand, an analog piece of equipment, or a digital process and/or processor. One of the most important aspects of algorithm design is creating an algorithm that has an efficient run time, also known as its big Oh.

Famous Algorithms

- Dijkstra's algorithm

- Kruskal's algorithm
- Quicksort
- Merge sort
- Depth-first search
- Breadth-first search
- Insertion sort

ALGORITHM ENGINEERING

Algorithm engineering is a combination of theoretical algorithm design with real-world data. By taking an algorithm and combining it with a hardware device connected to the real world, you are able to more accurately verify and validate the algorithm results and behaviour. The real-world device may be a simple data acquisition or stimulus device or you may take the algorithm and implement it on some embedded platform such as an FPGA or microprocessor that may be similar to the final system design. The term "algorithm engineering" was first used with specificity in 1997, with the organization of the first Workshop on Algorithm Engineering (WAE97). It has recently been used to help describe the steps in graphical system design: "a modern approach to designing, prototyping, and deploying embedded systems that combines open graphical programming with COTS hardware to dramatically simplify development, resulting in higher-quality designs with a migration to custom design". An article from Embedded.com that discusses algorithm engineering with respect to ESL. Algorithm engineering refers to the process required to transform a pencil-and-paper algorithm into a robust, efficient, well tested, and easily usable implementation. Thus it encompasses a number of topics, from modeling cache behaviour to the principles of good software engineering; its main focus, however, is experimentation. (Algorithm Engineering for Parallel Computation; David A. Bader, Bernard M. E. Moret, and Peter Sanders)

Conferences

Some annual conferences have been held for algorithm engineering:

- Workshop on Algorithm Engineering (WAE), since 1997.
- Workshop on Algorithm Engineering and Experimentation (ALENEX), since 1999.

The 1997 Workshop on Algorithm Engineering (WAE'97) was held in Venice (Italy) on September 11–13, 1997. The Third International Workshop on Algorithm Engineering (WAE'99) was held in London, UK in July 1999. The first Workshop on Algorithm Engineering and Experimentation (ALENEX99) was held in Baltimore, Maryland on January 15–16, 1999. It was sponsored by DIMACS, the Center for Discrete Mathematics and Theoretical Computer Science (at Rutgers University), with additional support from SIGACT, the ACM Special Interest Group on Algorithms and Computation Theory, and SIAM, the Society for Industrial and Applied Mathematics.

REFERENCES

Algorithm Design Paradigms - Overview by Paul Dunne at the University of Liverpool

Algorithm engineering: 3rd International Workshop, Jeffrey Scott Vitter, Christos D. Zaroliagis, 1999, web: BGoogle-sC.

Goodrich, Michael T.; Tamassia, Roberto (2002), *Algorithm Design: Foundations, Analysis, and Internet Examples*, John Wiley & Sons, Inc., ISBN 0-471-38365-1, http://ww3.algorithmdesign.net/ch00-front.html .

Jan van Leeuwen, ed. "Handbook of Theoretical Computer Science. Volume A: Algorithms and Complexity, *The MIT PRESS / Elsevier, 1990. ISBN 0-444-88071-2 (volume A). QA 76.H279 1990.*

Peter van Emde Boas, *Machine Models and Simulations* pp. 3–66, appearing in:

Stony Brook Algorithm Repository by Steven S. Skiena, Department of Computer Science, State University of New York.

3

Algorithm Efficiency, Synthesis and Programme Optimization

ALGORITHMIC EFFICIENCY

In computer science, efficiency is used to describe properties of an algorithm relating to how much of various types of resources it consumes. Algorithmic efficiency can be thought of as analogous to engineering productivity for a repeating or continuous process, where the goal is to reduce resource consumption, including time to completion, to some acceptable, optimal level.

Software Metrics

The two most frequently encountered and measurable metrics of an algorithm are:-

- speed or running time - the time it takes for an algorithm to complete, and
- 'space' - the memory or 'non-volatile storage' used by the algorithm during its operation.

but also might apply to

- transmission size - such as required bandwidth during normal operation or
- size of external memory- such as temporary disk space used to accomplish its task

and perhaps even

- the size of required 'longterm' disk space required after its operation to record its output or maintain its required function during its required useful lifetime (examples: a data table, archive or a computer log) and also
- the performance per watt and the total energy, consumed by the chosen hardware implementation (with its System requirements, necessary auxiliary support systems including interfaces, cabling, switching, cooling and security), during its required useful lifetime. See Total cost of ownership for other potential costs that might be associated with any particular implementation.

(An extreme example of these metrics might be to consider their values in relation to a repeated simple algorithm for calculating and storing (ð+n) to 50 decimal places running for say, 24 hours, either on a "pocket calculator" sized processor such as an ipod or an early mainframe operating in its own purpose-built heated or air conditioned unit.) The process of making code more efficient is known as optimization and in the case of automatic optimization (i.e. compiler optimization - performed by compilers on request or by default), usually focus on space at the cost of speed, or vice versa.

There are also quite simple programming techniques and 'avoidance strategies' that can actually improve both at the same time, usually irrespective of hardware, software or language. Even the re-ordering of nested conditional statements - to put the least frequently occurring condition first (example: test patients for blood type ='AB-', before testing age > 18, since this type of blood occurs in only about 1 in 100 of the population - thereby eliminating the second test at runtime in 99% of instances), can reduce actual instruction path length, something an optimizing compiler would almost certainly not be aware of - but which a programmer can research relatively easily even without specialist medical knowledge.

History

The first machines that were capable of computation were severely limited by purely mechanical considerations. As later electronic machines were developed they were, in turn, limited by the speed of their electronic counterparts. As software replaced hard-wired circuits, the efficiency of algorithms also became important. It has long been recognized that the precise 'arrangement of processes' is critical in reducing elapse time.

- "In almost every computation a great variety of arrangements for the succession of the processes is possible, and various considerations must influence the selections amongst them for the purposes of a calculating engine. One essential object is to choose that arrangement which shall tend to reduce to a minimum the time necessary for completing the calculation"

Ada Lovelace 1815-1852, generally considered as 'the first programmer' who worked on Charles Babbage's early mechanical general-purpose computer

- "In established engineering disciplines a 12% improvement, easily obtained, is never considered marginal and I believe the same viewpoint should prevail in software engineering"

Extract from "Structured Programming with go to Statements" by Donald Knuth, renowned computer scientist and Professor Emeritus of the Art of Computer Programming at Stanford University.

- "The key to performance is elegance, not battalions of special cases" attributed to Jon Bentley and (Malcolm) Douglas McIlroy

Speed

The absolute speed of an algorithm for a given input can simply be measured as the duration of execution (or clock time) and the results can be averaged over several executions to eliminate possible random effects. Most modern processors operate in a multi-processing & multi-programming environment so consideration must be made for parallel processes occurring on the same physical machine, eliminating these as far as possible. For superscalar processors, the speed of a given algorithm can sometimes be improved through instruction-level parallelism within a single processor (but, for optimal results, the algorithm may require some adaptation to this environment to gain significant advantage ('speedup'), becoming, in effect, an entirely different algorithm). A relative measure of an algorithms performance can sometimes be gained from the total instruction path length which can be determined by a run time Instruction Set Simulator (where available). An estimate of the speed of an algorithm can be determined in various ways. The most common method uses time complexity to determine the Big-O of an algorithm. See Run-time analysis for estimating how fast a particular algorithm may be according to its type (example: lookup unsorted list, lookup sorted list etc.) and in terms of scalability - its dependence on 'size of input', processor power and other factors.

Memory

Often, it is possible to make an algorithm faster at the expense of memory. This might be the case whenever the result of an 'expensive' calculation is cached rather than recalculating it afresh each time. The additional memory requirement would, in this case, be considered additional overhead although, in many situations, the stored result occupies very little extra space and can often be held in pre-compiled static storage, reducing not just processing time but also allocation & deallocation of working memory.

This is a very common method of improving speed, so much so that some programming languages often add special features to support it, such as C++'s 'mutable' keyword. The memory requirement of an algorithm is actually two separate but related things:-

- The memory taken up by the compiled executable code (the object code or binary file) itself (on disk or equivalent, depending on the hardware and language). This can often be reduced by preferring run-time decision making mechanisms (such as virtual functions and run-time type information) over certain compile-time decision making mechanisms (such as macro substitution and templates). This, however, comes at the cost of speed.
- Amount of temporary "dynamic memory" allocated during processing. For example, dynamically pre-caching results, as mentioned earlier, improves speed at the cost of this attribute. Even the depth of sub-routine calls can impact heavily on this cost and increase path length too, especially if there are 'heavy' dynamic memory requirements for the particular functions invoked. The use of copied function parameters (rather than simply using pointers to earlier, already defined, and sometimes static values) actually doubles the memory requirement for this particular memory metric (as well as carrying its own processing overhead for the copying itself. This can be particularly relevant for quite 'lengthy' parameters such as html script, JavaScript source programmes or extensive freeform text such as letters or emails.

Rematerialization

It has been argued that Rematerialization (re-calculating) may occasionally be more efficient than holding results in cache. This is the somewhat non-intuitive belief that it can be faster to re-calculate from the input - even if the answer is already known - when it can be shown, in some special cases, to decrease "register pressure". Some optimizing compilers have the ability to decide when this is considered worthwhile based on a number of criteria such as complexity and no side effects, and works by keeping track of the expression used to compute each variable, using the concept of available expressions. This is most likely to be true when a calculation is very fast (such as addition or bitwise operations), while the amount of data which must be cached would be very large, resulting in inefficient storage. Small amounts of data can be stored very efficiently in registers or fast cache, while in most contemporary computers large amounts of data must be stored in slower memory or even slower hard drive storage, and thus the efficiency of storing data which can be computed quickly drops significantly.

Precomputation

Precomputing a complete range of results prior to compiling, or at the beginning of an algorithm's execution, can often increase algorithmic efficiency substantially. This becomes advantageous when one or more inputs is constrained to a small enough range that the results can be stored in a reasonably sized block of memory. Because memory access is essentially constant in time complexity (except for caching delays), any algorithm with a component which has worse than constant efficiency over a small input range can be improved by precomputing values. In some cases efficient approximation algorithms can be obtained by computing a discrete subset of values and interpolating for intermediate input values, since interpolation is also a linear operation.

Transmission Size

Data compression algorithms can be useful because they help reduce the consumption of expensive resources, such as hard disk space or transmission bandwidth. This however also comes at a cost - which is additional processing time to compress and subsequently decompress. Depending upon the speed of the data transfer, compression may reduce overall response times which, ultimately, equates to speed - even though processing within the computer itself takes longer. For audio, MP3 is a compression method used extensively in portable sound systems. The efficiency of a data compression algorithm relates to the compression factor and speed of achieving both compression and decompression. For the purpose of archiving an extensive database, it might be considered worthwhile to achieve a very high compression ratio, since decompression is less likely to occur on the majority of the data.

Data Presentation

Output data can be presented to the end user in many ways - such as via punched tape or card, digital displays, local display monitors, remote computer monitors or printed. Each of these has its own inherent initial cost and, in some cases, an ongoing cost (e.g. refreshing an image from memory). As an example, the web site "Google" recently showed, as its logo, an image of the Vancouver olympics that is around 8K of gif image. The normally displayed Google image is a PNG image of 28K (or 48K), yet the raw text string for "Google" occupies only 6 octets or 48 bits (4,778 or 8192 *times* less). This graphically illustrates that how data is presented can significantly effect the overall efficiency of transmission (and also the complete algorithm - since both GIF and PNG images require yet more processing). It is estimated by "Internet World Stats" that there were 1,733,993,741 internet users in 2009 and, to transmit this new image to each one of them, would require around 136,000 *billion* (10^9)octets of data to be transmitted - at least once - into their personal web cache. In "Computational Energy Cost of TCP", co-authors Bokyung Wang and Suresh Singh examine the energy costs for TCP and calculated, for their chosen example, a cost of 0.022 Joules per packet (of approx 1489 octets). On this basis, a total of around 2,000,000,000 joules (2 GJ) of energy might be expended by TCP elements alone to display the new logo for all users for the first time. To maintain or re-display this image requires still more processing and consequential energy cost (in contrast to printed output for instance).

Encoding and Decoding Methods (Compared and Contrasted)

When data is encoded for any 'external' use, it is possible to do so in an almost unlimited variety of different formats that are sometimes conflicting. This content encoding (of the raw data) may be designed for:

- optimal readability – by humans
- optimal decoding speed – by other computer programmes
- optimal compression – for archiving or data transmission
- optimal compatibility – with "legacy" or other existing formats or programming languages
- optimal security – using encryption

  (For character level encoding, see the various encoding techniques such as EBCDIC or ASCII)

It is unlikely that all of these goals could be met with a single 'generic' encoding scheme and so a compromise will often be the desired goal and will often be compromised by the need for standardization and/or legacy and compatibility issues.

Encoding Efficiently

For data encoding whose destination is to be input for further computer processing, readability is not an issue – since the receiving processors algorithm can decode the data to any other desirable form including human readable. From the perspective of algorithmic efficiency, minimizing subsequent decoding (with zero or minimal parsing) should take highest priority. The general rule of thumb is that any encoding system that 'understands' the underlying data structure - sufficiently to encode it in the first place - should be equally capable of easily encoding it in such a way that makes decoding it highly efficient. For variable length data with possibly omitted data values, for instance, this almost certainly means the utilization of declarative notation (i.e. including the length of the data item as a prefix to the data so that a de-limiter is not required and parsing completely eliminated). For keyword data items, tokenizing the key to an index (integer) after its first occurrence not only reduces subsequent data size but, furthermore, reduces future decoding overhead for the same items that are repeated. For more 'generic' encoding for efficient data compression see Arithmetic encoding and entropy encoding articles.

Historically, optimal encoding was not only worthwhile from an efficiency standpoint but was also common practise to conserve valuable memory, external storage and processor resources. Once validated a country name for example could be held as a shorter sequential country code which could then also act as an index for subsequent 'decoding', using this code as an entry number within a table or record number within a file. If the table or file contained fixed length entries, the code could easily be converted to an absolute memory address or disk address for fast retrieval. The ISBN system for identifying books is a good example of a practical encoding method which also contains a built-in hierarchy. According to recent articles in New Scientist and Scientific American; "TODAY'S telecommunications networks could use one ten-thousandth of the power they presently consume if smarter data-coding techniques were used", according to Bell Labs, based in Murray Hill, New Jersey It recognizes that this is only a theoretical limit but nevertheless sets itself a more realistic, practical goal of a 1,000 fold reduction within 5 years with future, as yet unidentified, technological changes.

Examples of Several Common Encoding Methods

- Comma separated values (CSV - a list of data values separated by commas)
- Tab separated values (TSV) - a list of data values separated by 'tab' characters
- HyperText Markup Language (HTML) - the predominant markup language for web pages
- Extensible Markup Language (XML) - a generic framework for storing any amount of text or any data whose structure can be represented as a tree with at least one element - the root element.
- JavaScript Object Notation (JSON) - human-readable format for representing simple data structures

The last of these, (JSON) is apparently widely used for internet data transmission, primarily it seems because the data can be uploaded by a single JavaScript 'eval' statement - without the need to produce what otherwise would likely have been a more efficient purpose built encoder/decoder. There are in fact quite large amounts of repeated (and therefore redundant data) in this particular format, and also in HTML and XML source, that could quite easily be eliminated. XML is recognized as a verbose form of encoding. Binary XML has been put forward as one method of reducing transfer and processing times for XML and, while there are several competing formats, none has been widely adopted by a standards organization or accepted as a de facto standard. It has also been criticized by Jimmy Zhang for essentially trying to solve the wrong problem There are a number of freely available products on the market that partially compress HTML files and perform some or all of the following:

- merge lines
- remove unnecessary whitespace characters
- remove unnecessary quotation marks. For example, BORDER="0" will be replaced with BORDER=0)
- replace some tags with shorter ones (e.g. replace STRIKE tags with S, STRONG with B and EM with I)
- remove HTML comments (comments within scripts and styles are not removed)
- remove <!DOCTYPE..> tags
- remove named meta tags

The effect of this limited form of compression is to make the HTML code smaller and faster to load, but more difficult to read manually (so the original HTML code is usually retained for updating), but since it is predominantly meant to be processed only by a browser, this causes no problems. Despite these small improvements, HTML, which is the predominant language for the web still remains a predominantly *source* distributed, interpreted markup language, with high redundancy.

Kolmogorov Complexity

The study of encoding techniques has been examined in depth in an area of computer science characterized by a method known as Kolmogorov complexity where a value known as ('K') is accepted as 'not a computable function'. The Kolmogorov complexity of any computable object is the length of the shortest programme that computes it and then halts. The invariance theorem shows that it is not really important which computer is used. Essentially this implies that there is no automated method that can produce an optimum result and is therefore characterized by a requirement for human ingenuity or Innovation. See also Algorithmic probability.

Effect of Programming Paradigms

The effect that different programming paradigms have on algorithmic efficiency is fiercely contested, with both supporters and antagonists for each new paradigm. Strong supporters of structured programming, such as Dijkstra for instance, who favour entirely goto-less programmes are met with conflicting evidence that appears to nullify its supposed benefits. The truth is, even if the structured code itself contains no gotos, the optimizing compiler that creates the binary code almost certainly generates them (and not necessarily in the most efficient way). Similarly, OOP protagonists who claim their paradigm is superior are met with opposition from strong sceptics such as Alexander Stepanov who suggested that OOP provides a mathematically limited viewpoint and called it, "almost as much of a hoax as Artificial Intelligence" In the long term, benchmarks, using real-life examples, provide the only real hope of resolving such conflicts - at least in terms of run-time efficiency.

Optimization Techniques

The word optimize is normally used in relation to an existing algorithm/computer programme (i.e. to improve upon completed code). In this section it is used both in the context of existing programmes and also in the design and implementation of new algorithms, thereby avoiding the most common performance pitfalls. It is clearly wasteful to produce a working programme - at first using an algorithm that ignores all efficiency issues - only to then have to redesign or rewrite sections of it if found to offer poor performance. Optimization can be broadly categorized into two domains:-

- Environment specific - that are essentially worthwhile only on certain platforms or particular computer languages

- General techniques - that apply irrespective of platform

Environment Specific

Optimization of algorithms frequently depends on the properties of the machine the algorithm will be executed on as well as the language the algorithm is written in and chosen data types. For example, a programmer might optimize code for time efficiency in an application for home computers (with sizable amounts of memory), but for code destined to be embedded in small, "memory-tight" devices, the programmer may have to accept that it will run more slowly, simply because of the restricted memory available for any potential software optimization. For a discussion of hardware performance, see article on Computer performance which covers such things as CPU clock speed, cycles per instruction and other relevant metrics. For a discussion on how the choice of particular instructions available on a specific machine effect efficiency, see later section 'Choice of instruction and data type'.

General Techniques

- Linear search such as unsorted table look-ups in particular can be very expensive in terms of execution time but can be reduced significantly through use of efficient techniques such as indexed arrays and binary searches. Using a simple linear search on first occurrence and using a cached result thereafter is an obvious compromise.
- Use of indexed programme branching, utilizing branch tables or "threaded code" to control programme flow, (rather than using multiple conditional IF statements or unoptimized CASE/ SWITCH) can drastically reduce instruction path length, simultaneously reduce programme size and even also make a programme easier to read and

more easily maintainable (in effect it becomes a 'decision table' rather than repetitive spaghetti code).

- Loop unrolling performed manually, or more usually by an optimizing compiler, can provide significant savings in some instances. By processing 'blocks' of several array elements at a time, individually addressed, (for example, within a While loop), much pointer arithmetic and end of loop testing can be eliminated, resulting in decreased instruction path lengths. Other Loop optimizations are also possible.

Tunnel Vision

There are many techniques for improving algorithms, but focusing on a single favourite technique can lead to a "tunnel vision" mentality. For example, in this X86 assembly example, the author offers loop unrolling as a reasonable technique that provides some 40% improvements to his chosen example. However, the same example would benefit significantly from both inlining and use of a trivial hash function. If they were implemented, either as alternative or complementary techniques, an even greater percentage gain might be expected. A combination of optimizations may provide ever increasing speed, but selection of the most easily implemented and most effective technique, from a large repertoire of such techniques, is desirable as a starting point.

Dependency Trees and Spreadsheets

Spreadsheets are a 'special case' of algorithms that self-optimize by virtue of their dependency trees that are inherent in the design of spreadsheets to reduce re-calculations when a cell changes. The results of earlier calculations are effectively cached within the workbook and only updated if another cells changed value effects it directly.

Table Lookup

Table lookups can make many algorithms more efficient, particularly when used to bypass computations with a high time complexity. However, if a wide input range is required, they can consume significant storage resources. In cases with a sparse valid input set, hash functions can be used to provide more efficient lookup access than a full table.

Hash Function Algorithms

A hash function is any well-defined procedure or mathematical function which converts a large, possibly variable-sized amount of data into a small datum, usually a single integer that may serve as an index to an array. The values returned by a hash function are called hash values, hash codes, hash sums, or simply hashes. Hash functions are frequently used to speed up table lookups. The choice of a hashing function (to avoid a linear or brute force search) depends critically on the nature of the input data, and their probability distribution in the intended application.

Trivial Hash Function

Sometimes if the datum is small enough, a "trivial hash function" can be used to effectively provide constant time searches at almost zero cost. This is particularly relevant for single byte lookups (e.g. ASCII or EBCDIC characters)

Searching Strings

Searching for particular text strings (for instance "tags" or keywords) in long sequences of characters potentially generates lengthy instruction paths. This includes searching for delimiters in comma separated files or similar processing which can be very simply and effectively eliminated (using declarative notation for instance). Several methods of reducing the cost for general searching have been examined and the “Boyer–Moore string search algorithm” (or Boyer–Moore–Horspool algorithm, a similar but modified version) is one solution that has been proven to give superior results to repetitive comparisons of the entire search string along the sequence.

Hot Spot Analyzers

Special system software products known as “performance analyzers” are often available from suppliers to help diagnose “hot spots” - during actual execution of computer programmes - using real or test data - they perform a Performance analysis under generally repeatable conditions. They can pinpoint sections of the programme that might benefit from specifically targeted programmer optimization without necessarily spending time optimizing the rest of the code. Using programme re-runs, a measure of relative improvement can then be determined to decide if the optimization was successful and by what amount. Instruction Set Simulators can be used as an alternative to measure the instruction path length at the machine code level between selected execution paths, or on the entire execution. Regardless of the type of tool used, the quantitative values obtained can be used in combination with anticipated reductions (for the targeted code) to estimate a relative or absolute overall saving. For example if 50% of the total execution time (or path length) is absorbed in a subroutine whose speed can be doubled by programmer optimization, an overall saving of around 25% might be expected (Amdahl law). Efforts have been made at the University of California, Irvine to produce dynamic executable code using a combination of hot spot analysis and run-time programme trace tree. A JIT like dynamic compiler was built by Andreas Gal and others, “in which relevant (i.e., frequently executed) control flows are ...discovered lazily during execution”

Benchmarking & Competitive Algorithms

For new versions of software or to provide comparisons

with competitive systems, benchmarks are sometimes used which assist with gauging an algorithms relative performance. If a new sort algorithm is produced for example it can be compared with its predecessors to ensure that at least it is efficient as before with known data - taking into consideration any functional improvements. Benchmarks can be used by customers when comparing various products from alternative suppliers to estimate which product will best suit their specific requirements in terms of functionality and performance. For example in the mainframe world certain proprietary sort products from independent software companies such as Syncsort compete with products from the major suppliers such as IBM for speed. Some benchmarks provide opportunities for producing an analysis comparing the relative speed of various compiled and interpreted languages for example and *The Computer Language Benchmarks Game* compares the performance of implementations of typical programming problems in several programming languages. (Even creating "do it yourself" benchmarks to get at least some appreciation of the relative performance of different programming languages, using a variety of user specified criteria, is quite simple to produce as this "Nine language Performance roundup" by Christopher W. Cowell-Shah demonstrates by example)

Compiled Versus Interpreted Languages

A compiled algorithm will, in general, execute faster than the equivalent interpreted algorithm simply because some processing is required even at run time to 'understand' (i.e. interpret) the instructions to effect an execution. A compiled programme will normally output an object or machine code equivalent of the algorithm that has already been processed by the compiler into a form more readily executed by microcode or the hardware directly. The popular Perl language is an example of an interpreted language and benchmarks indicate that it executes approximately 24 times more slowly than compiled C.

Optimizing Compilers

Many compilers have features that attempt to optimize the code they generate, utilizing some of the techniques outlined in this study and others specific to the compilation itself. Loop optimization is often the focus of optimizing compilers because significant time is spent in programme loops and parallel processing opportunities can often be facilitated by automatic code re-structuring such as loop unrolling. Optimizing compilers are by no means perfect. There is no way that a compiler can guarantee that, for all programme source code, the fastest (or smallest) possible equivalent compiled programme is output; such a compiler is fundamentally impossible because it would solve the halting problem. Additionally, even optimizing compilers generally have no access to runtime metrics to enable them to improve optimization through 'learning'.

Just-in-Time Compilers

'On-the-fly' processors known today as just-in-time or 'JIT' compilers combine features of interpreted languages with compiled languages and may also incorporate elements of optimization to a greater or lesser extent. Essentially the JIT compiler can compile small sections of source code statements (or bytecode) as they are newly encountered and (usually) retain the result for the next time the same source is processed. In addition, pre-compiled segments of code can be in-lined or called as dynamic functions that themselves perform equally fast as the equivalent 'custom' compiled function. Because the JIT processor also has access to run-time information (that a normal compiler can't have) it is also possible for it to optimize further executions depending upon the input and also perform other run-time introspective optimization as execution proceeds. A JIT processor may, or may not, incorporate self modifying code or its equivalent by creating 'fast path' routes through an algorithm. It may also use such techniques as dynamic Fractional cascading or any other similar runtime device based on collected actual runtime metrics. It is therefore entirely possible that a JIT compiler might (counter intuitively) execute even faster than an optimally 'optimized' compiled programme.

Self-Modifying Code

As mentioned above, just-in-time compilers often make extensive use of self-modifying code to generate the actual machine instructions required to be executed. The technique can also be used to reduce instruction path lengths in application programmes where otherwise repetitive conditional tests might otherwise be required within the main programme flow. This can be particularly useful where a sub routine may have embedded debugging code that is either active (testing mode) or inactive (production mode) depending upon some input parameter. A simple solution using a form of dynamic dispatching is where the sub routine entry point is dynamically 'swapped' at initialization, depending upon the input parameter. Entry point A) includes the debugging code prologue and entry point B) excludes the prologue; thus eliminating all overhead except the initial 'test and swap' (even when test/debugging is selected, when the overhead is simply the test/debugging code itself).

Genetic Algorithm

In the world of performance related algorithms it is worth mentioning the role of genetic algorithms which compete using similar methods to the natural world in eliminating inferior algorithms in favour of more efficient versions.

Object Code Optimizers

Some proprietary programme optimizers such as the "COBOL Optimizer" developed by Capex Corporation in the mid 1970's for COBOL, actually took the unusual step of optimizing the Object code (or binary file) after normal compilation. This type of optimizer, recently sometimes referred to as a "post pass" optimizer or peephole optimizer, depended, in this case, upon knowledge of 'weaknesses' in the standard IBM COBOL compiler and actually replaced (or patched) sections of the object code with more efficient code. A number of other suppliers have recently adopted the same approach.

Alignment of Data

Most processors execute faster if certain data values are aligned on word, doubleword or page boundaries. If possible design/specify structures to satisfy appropriate alignments. This avoids exceptions.

Locality of Reference

To reduce Cache miss exceptions by providing good spatial locality of reference, specify 'high frequency'/volative working storage data within defined structure(s) so that they are also allocated from contiguous sections of memory (rather than possibly scattered over many pages). Group closely related data values also 'physically' close together within these structures. Consider the possibility of creating an 'artificial' structure to group some otherwise unrelated, but nevertheless frequently referenced, items together.

Choice of Instruction or Data Type

Particularly in an Assembly language (although also applicable to HLL statements), the choice of a particular 'instruction' or data type, can have a large impact on execution efficiency. In general, instructions that process variables such as signed or unsigned 16-bit or 32-bit integers are faster than those that process floating point or packed decimal. Modern processors are even capable of executing multiple 'fixed point' instructions in parallel with the simultaneous execution of a floating point instruction. If the largest integer to be encountered can be accommodated by the 'faster' data type, defining the variables as that type will result in faster execution - since even a non-optimizing compiler will, in-effect, be 'forced' to choose appropriate instructions that will execute faster than would have been the case with data types associated with 'slower' instructions. Assembler programmers (and optimizing compiler writers) can then also benefit from the ability to perform certain common types of arithmetic for instance - division by 2, 4, 8 etc. by performing the very much faster binary shift right operations (in this case by 1, 2 or 3 bits). If the choice of input data type is not under the control of the programmer, although prior conversion (outside of a loop for instance) to a faster data type carries some overhead, it can often be worthwhile if the variable is then to be used as a loop counter, especially if the count could be quite a high value or there are many input values to process. As mentioned above, choice of individual assembler instructions (or even sometimes just their order of execution) on particular machines can effect the efficiency of an algorithm. See Assembly Optimization Tips for one quite numerous arcane list of various technical (and sometimes non-intuitive) considerations for choice of assembly instructions on different processors that also discusses the merits of each case. Sometimes microcode or hardware quirks can result in unexpected performance differences between processors that assembler programmers can actively code for - or else specifically avoid if penalties result - something even the best optimizing compiler may not be designed to handle.

Data Granularity

The greater the granularity of data definitions (such as splitting a geographic address into separate street/city/postal code fields) can have performance overhead implications during processing. Higher granularity in this example implies more procedure calls in Object-oriented programming and parallel computing environments since the additional objects are accessed via multiple method calls rather than perhaps one.

Subroutine Granularity

For structured programming and procedural programming in general, great emphasis is placed on designing programmes as a hierarchy of (or at least a set of) subroutines. For object oriented programming, the method call (a subroutine call) is the standard method of testing and setting all values in objects and so increasing data granularity consequently causes increased use of subroutines. The greater the granularity of subroutine usage, the larger the proportion of processing time devoted to the mechanism of the subroutine linkages themselves.The presence of a (called) subroutine in a programme contributes nothing extra to the functionality of the programme. The extent to which subroutines (and their consequent memory requirements) influences the overall performance of the complete algorithm depends to a large extent on the actual implementation. In assembly language programmes, the invocation of a subroutine need not involve much overhead, typically adding just a couple of machine instructions to the normal instruction path length, each one altering the control flow either *to* the subroutine or returning *from* it (saving the state on a stack being optional, depending on the complexity of the subroutine and its requirement to reuse general purpose registers). In many cases, small subroutines that perform frequently used data transformations using 'general purpose' work areas can be accomplished without the need to save or restore any registers, including the return register.

By contrast, HLL programmes typically always invoke a 'standard' procedure call (the *calling convention*), which involves saving the programme state by default and usually allocating additional memory on the stack to save all registers and other relevant state data (the prologue and epilogue code). Recursion in a HLL programme can consequently consume significant overhead in both memory and execution time managing the stack to the required depth. Guy Steele pointed out in a 1977 paper that a *well-designed* programming language implementation *can* have very low overheads for procedural abstraction (but laments, in most implementations, that they seldom achieve this in practice - being "rather thoughtless or careless in this regard"). Steele concludes that "we should have a healthy respect for procedure calls" (because they are powerful) but he also cautioned "use them sparingly" See section Avoiding costs for discussion of how inlining subroutines can be used to improve performance. For the Java language, use of the "final" keyword can be used to force method inlining (resulting in elimination of the method call, no dynamic dispatch and the possibility to constant-fold the value - with no code executed at runtime)

Choice of Language / Mixed Languages

Some computer languages can execute algorithms more efficiently than others. As stated already, interpreted languages often perform less efficiently than compiled languages. In addition, where possible, 'high-use', and time-dependent sections of code may be written in a language such as assembler that can usually execute faster and make better use of resources on a particular platform than the equivalent HLL code on the same platform. This section of code can either be statically called or dynamically invoked (external function) or embedded within the higher level code (e.g. Assembler instructions embedded in a 'C' language program). The effect of higher levels of abstraction when using a HLL has been described as the *Abstraction penalty* Programmers who are familiar with assembler language (in addition to their chosen HLL) and are also familiar with the code that will be generated by the HLL, under known conditions, can sometimes use HLL language primitives of that language to generate code almost identical to assembler language. This is most likely to be possible only in languages that support pointers such as PL/1 or C. This is facilitated if the chosen HLL compiler provides an optional assembler listing as part of its printout so that various alternatives can be explored without also needing specialist knowledge of the compiler internals.

Software Validation Versus Hardware Validation

An optimization technique that was frequently taken advantage of on 'legacy' platforms was that of allowing the hardware (or microcode) to perform validation on numeric data fields such as those coded in (or converted to) packed decimal (or packed BCD). The choice was to either spend processing time checking each field for a valid numeric content in the particular internal representation chosen or simply assume the data was correct and let the hardware detect the error upon execution. The choice was highly significant because to check for validity on multiple fields (for sometimes many millions of input records), it could occupy valuable computer resources. Since input data fields were in any case frequently built from the output of earlier computer processing, the actual probability of a field containing invalid data was exceedingly low and usually the result of some 'corruption'. The solution was to incorporate an 'event handler' for the hardware detected condition ('data exception)' that would intercept the occasional errant data field and either 'report, correct and continue' or, more usually, abort the run with a core dump to try to determine the reason for the bad data.

Similar event handlers are frequently utilized in today's web based applications to handle other exceptional conditions but repeatedly parsing data input, to ensure its validity before execution, has nevertheless become much more commonplace - partly because processors have become faster (and the perceived need for efficiency in this area less significant) but, predominantly - because data structures have become less 'formalized' (e.g. .csv and .tsv files) or uniquely identifiable (e.g. packed decimal). The potential savings using this type of technique may have therefore fallen into general dis-use as a consequence and therefore repeated data validations and repeated data conversions have become an accepted overhead. Ironically, one consequence of this move to less formalized data structures is that a corruption of say, a numeric binary integer value, will not be detected at all by the hardware upon execution (for instance: is an ASCII hexadecimal value '20202020' a valid signed or unsigned binary value - or simply a string of blanks that has corrupted it?)

Algorithms for Vector & Superscalar Processors

Algorithms for vector processors are usually different than those for scalar processors since they can process multiple instructions and/or multiple data elements in parallel. The process of converting an algorithm from a scalar to a vector process is known as vectorization and methods for automatically performing this transformation as efficiently as possible are constantly sought. There are intrinsic limitations for implementing instruction level parallelism in Superscalar processors but, in essence, the overhead in deciding for certain if particular instruction sequences can be processed in parallel can sometimes exceed the efficiency gain in so doing. The achievable reduction is governed primarily by the (somewhat obvious) law known as Amdahl's law, that essentially states that the improvement from parallel processing is determined by its slowest sequential component. Algorithms designed for this class of processor therefore require more care if they are not to unwittingly disrupt the potential gains.

Avoiding Costs

- Defining variables as integers for indexed arrays instead of floating point will result in faster execution.
- Defining structures whose structure length is a multiple of a power of 2 (2,4,8,16 etc.), will allow the compiler to calculate array indexes by shifting a binary index by 1, 2 or more bits to the left,

instead of using a multiply instruction will result in faster execution. Adding an otherwise redundant short filler variable to 'pad out' the length of a structure element to say 8 bytes when otherwise it would have been 6 or 7 bytes may reduce overall processing time by a worthwhile amount for very large arrays. See for generated code differences for C as for example.

- Storage defined in terms of bits, when bytes would suffice, may inadvertently involve extremely long path lengths involving bitwise operations instead of more efficient single instruction 'multiple byte' copy instructions. (This does not apply to 'genuine' intentional bitwise operations - used for example instead of multiplication or division by powers of 2 or for TRUE/FALSE flags.)
- Unnecessary use of allocated dynamic storage when static storage would suffice, can increase the processing overhead substantially - both increasing memory requirements and the associated allocation/deallocation path length overheads for each function call.
- Excessive use of function calls for very simple functions, rather than in-line statements, can also add substantially to instruction path lengths and stack/unstack overheads. For particularly time critical systems that are not also code size sensitive, automatic or manual inline expansion can reduce path length by eliminating all the instructions that call the function and return from it. (A conceptually similar method, loop unrolling, eliminates the instructions required to set up and terminate a loop by, instead; repeating the instructions inside the loop multiple times. This of course eliminates the branch back instruction but may also increase the size of the binary file or, in the

case of JIT built code, dynamic memory. Also, care must be taken with this method, that re-calculating addresses for each statement within an unwound indexed loop is not more expensive than incrementing pointers within the former loop would have been. If absolute indexes are used in the generated (or manually created) unwound code, rather than variables, the code created may actually be able to avoid generated pointer arithmetic instructions altogether, using offsets instead).

Memory Management

Whenever memory is *automatically* allocated (for example in HLL programmes, when calling a procedure or when issuing a system call), it is normally released (or 'freed'/ 'deallocated'/ 'deleted') automatically when it is no longer required - thus allowing it to be re-used for another purpose *immediately*. Some memory management can easily be accomplished by the compiler, as in this example. However, when memory is *explicitly* allocated (for example in OOP when "new" is specified for an object), releasing the memory is often left to an asynchronous 'garbage collector' which does not necessarily release the memory at the earliest opportunity (as well as consuming some additional CPU resources deciding if it can be). The current trend nevertheless appears to be towards taking full advantage of this fully automated method, despite the tradeoff in efficiency - because it is claimed that it makes programming easier. Some functional languages are known as 'lazy functional languages' because of the significant use of garbage collection and can consume much more memory as a result.

- Array processing may simplify programming but use of separate statements to sum different elements of the same array(s) may produce code that is not easily optimized and that requires multiple passes of the arrays that might otherwise have been processed in a single pass. It may also duplicate data if array slicing is used, leading to increased memory usage and copying overhead.

- In OOP, if an object is known to be immutable, it can be copied simply by making a copy of a reference to it instead of copying the entire object. Because a reference (typically only the size of a pointer) is usually much smaller than the object itself, this results in memory savings and a boost in execution speed.

Readability, Trade Offs and Trends

One must be careful, in the pursuit of good coding style, not to over-emphasize efficiency. Frequently, a clean, readable and 'usable' design is much more important than a fast, efficient design that is hard to understand. There are exceptions to this 'rule' (such as embedded systems, where space is tight, and processing power minimal) but these are rarer than one might expect. However, increasingly, for many 'time critical' applications such as air line reservation systems, point-of-sale applications, ATMs (cash-point machines), Airline Guidance systems, Collision avoidance systems and numerous modern web based applications - operating in a real-time environment where speed of response is fundamental - there is little alternative.

Determining if Optimization is Worthwhile

The essential criteria for using optimized code are of course dependent upon the expected use of the algorithm. If it is a new algorithm and is going to be in use for many years and speed is relevant, it is worth spending some time designing the code to be as efficient as possible from the outset. If an existing algorithm is proving to be too slow or memory is becoming an issue, clearly something must be done to improve it. For the average application, or for one-off applications, avoiding inefficient coding techniques and encouraging the compiler to optimize where possible may be sufficient. One simple way (at least for mathematicians) to determine whether an optimization is worthwhile is as follows: Let the original time and space requirements (generally in Big-O notation) of the algorithm be O_1 and O_2. Let the new code require N_1 and N_2 time and space respectively. If $N_1N_2 < O_1O_2$, the optimization should be carried out. However, as mentioned above, this may not always be true.

Implications for Algorithmic Efficiency

A recent report, published in December 2007, from Global Action Plan, a UK-based environmental organization found that computer servers are "at least as great a threat to the climate as SUVs or the global aviation industry" drawing attention to the carbon footprint of the IT industry in the UK. According to an Environmental Research Letters report published in September 2008, "Total power used by information technology equipment in data centers represented about 0.5% of world electricity consumption in 2005. When cooling and auxiliary infrastructure are included, that figure is about 1%. The total data center power demand in 2005 is equivalent (in capacity terms) to about seventeen 1000 MW power plants for the world." Some media reports claim that performing two Google searches from a desktop computer can generate about the same amount of carbon dioxide as boiling a kettle for a cup of tea, according to new research; however, the factual accuracy of this comparison is disputed, and the author of the study in question asserts that the two-searches-tea-kettle statistic is a misreading of his work.

Greentouch, a recently established consortium of leading Information and Communications Technology (ICT) industry, academic and non-governmental research experts, has set itself the mission of reducing reduce energy consumption per user by a factor of 1000 from current levels. "A thousand-fold reduction is roughly equivalent to being able to power the world's communications networks, including the Internet, for three years using the same amount of energy that it currently takes to run them for a single day". The first meeting in February 2010 will establish the organization's five-year plan, first year deliverables and member roles and responsibilities. Intellectual property issues will be addressed and defined in the forum's initial planning meetings. The conditions for research and the results of that research will be high priority for discussion in the initial phase of the research forum's development. Computers having become increasingly more powerful over the past few decades, emphasis was on a 'brute force' mentality. This may have to be reconsidered in the light of these reports and more effort placed in future on reducing carbon footprints through optimization. It is a timely reminder that algorithmic efficiency is just another aspect of the more general thermodynamic efficiency. The genuine economic benefits of an optimized algorithm are, in any case, that more processing can be done for the same cost or that useful results can be shown in a more timely manner and ultimately, acted upon sooner.

Criticism of the Current State of Programming

- David May FRS a British computer scientist and currently Professor of Computer Science at University of Bristol and founder and CTO of XMOS Semiconductor, believes one of the problems is that there is a reliance on Moore's law to solve inefficiencies. He has advanced an 'alternative' to Moore's law (May's law) stated as follows:

Software efficiency halves every 18 months, compensating Moore's Law. In ubiquitous systems, halving the instructions executed can double the battery life and big data sets bring big opportunities for better software and algorithms: Reducing the number of operations from N x N to N x log(N) has a dramatic effect when N is large...

for N = 30 billion, this change is as good as 50 years of technology improvements

- Software author Adam N. Rosenburg in his blog "*The failure of the Digital computer*", has described the current state of programming as nearing the "Software event horizon", (alluding to the fictitious "*shoe event horizon*" described by Douglas Adams in his *Hitchhiker's Guide to the Galaxy* book). He estimates there has been a 70 dB factor loss of productivity or "99.99999 percent, of its ability to deliver the goods", since the 1980s - "When Arthur C. Clarke compared the reality of computing in 2001 to the computer HAL in his book 2001: A Space Odyssey, he pointed out how wonderfully small and powerful computers were but how disappointing computer programming had become".
- Conrad Weisert gives examples, some of which were published in ACM SIGPLAN (Special Interest Group on Programming Languages) Notices, December, 1995 in: "Atrocious Programming Thrives"

HIGH-LEVEL SYNTHESIS

High-level synthesis (HLS), sometimes referred to as *C synthesis, electronic system level (ESL) synthesis, algorithmic synthesis, or behavioural synthesis*, is an automated design process that interprets an algorithmic description of a desired behaviour and creates hardware that implements that behaviour. The starting point of a high-level synthesis flow is ANSI C/C++/SystemC code. The code is analyzed, architecturally constrained, and scheduled to create a register transfer level hardware design language (HDL), which is then in turn commonly synthesized to the gate level by the use of a logic synthesis tool. The goal of HLS is to let hardware designers efficiently build and verify hardware, by giving them better control over optimization of their design architecture, and through the nature of allowing the designer to describe the design at a higher level of tools while the tool does the RTL implementation. Verification of the RTL is an important part of the process.

Hardware design can be created at a variety of levels of abstraction. The commonly used levels of abstraction are gate level, register transfer level (RTL), and algorithmic level. While logic synthesis uses an RTL description of the design, high-level synthesis works at a higher level of abstraction, starting with an algorithmic description in a high-level language such as SystemC and Ansi C/C++. The designer typically develops the module functionality and the interconnect protocol. The high-level synthesis tools handle the micro-architecture and transform untimed or partially timed functional code into fully timed RTL implementations, automatically creating cycle-by-cycle detail for hardware implementation. The (RTL) implementations are then used directly in a conventional logic synthesis flow to create a gate-level implementation.

History

Early academic work extracted scheduling, allocation, and binding as the basic steps for high-level-synthesis. Scheduling partitions the algorithm in control steps that are used to define the states in the FSM. Each control step contains one small section of the algorithm that can be performed in a single clock cycle in the hardware. Allocation and binding maps the instructions and variables to the hardware components, multiplexors, registers and wires of the data path. First generation behavioural synthesis was introduced by Synopsys in 1994 as Behavioural Compiler and used Verilog or VHDL as input languages. The abstraction level used was partially timed (clocked) processes. Tools based on behavioural Verilog or VHDL were not widely adopted in part because neither languages nor the partially timed abstraction were well suited to modeling behaviour at a high level. 10 years later, in early 2004, Synopsys end-of-lifed Behavioural Compiler.

In 2004, there emerged a number of next generation commercial high-level synthesis products (also called behaviourial synthesis or algorithmic synthesis at the time) which provided synthesis of circuits specified at C level to a register transfer level (RTL) specification. Synthesizing from the popular C language offered accrued abstraction, expressive power and coding flexibility while tying with existing flows and legacy models. This language shift, combined with other technical advances was a key enabler for successful industrial usage. High-level synthesis tools are used for complex ASIC and FPGA design. High-level synthesis was primarily adopted in Japan and Europe in the early years. As of late 2008, there was an emerging adoption in the United States.

Source Input

The most common source inputs for high level synthesis are based on standards languages such as ANSI C/C++ and SystemC. High level synthesis typically also includes a bit-accurate executable specification as input, since to derive an efficient hardware implementation, additional information is needed on what is an acceptable Mean-Square Error or Bit-Error Rate etc. For example, if the designer starts with a FIR filter written using the "double" floating type, before he or she can derive an efficient hardware implementation, they need to perform numerical refinement to arrive at a fixed-point implementation. The refinement requires additional information on the level of quantization noise that can be tolerated, the valid input ranges etc. This bit-accurate specification makes the high level synthesis source specification functionally complete.

Process Stages

The high-level synthesis process consists of a number of activities. Various high-level synthesis tools perform these activities in different orders using different algorithms. Some high-level synthesis tools combine some of these activities or perform them iteratively to converge on the desired solution.

- *Lexical processing*
- *Algorithm optimization*
- *Control / Dataflow analysis*
- *Library processing*
- *Resource allocation*
- *Scheduling*
- *Functional unit binding*
- *Register binding*
- *Output processing*
- *Input rebundling*

Functionality

Architectural Constraints

Synthesis constraints for the architecture can automatically be applied based on the design analysis. These constraints can be broken into

- Hierarchy
- Interface
- Memory
- Loop
- Low-level timing constraints
- iteration

Interface Synthesis

Interface Synthesis refers to the ability to accept pure C/C++ description as its input, then use automated interface synthesis technology to control the timing and communications protocol on the design interface. This enables interface analysis and exploration of a full range of hardware interface options such as streaming, single- or dual-port RAM plus various handshaking mechanisms. With interface synthesis the designer does not embed interface protocols in the source description. Examples might be: direct connection, one line, 2 line handshake, FIFO.

PROGRAMME OPTIMIZATION

In computer science, programme optimization or software optimization is the process of modifying a software system to make some aspect of it work more efficiently or use fewer resources. In general, a computer programme may be optimized so that it executes more rapidly, or is capable of operating with less memory storage or other resources, or draw less power.

General

Although the word "optimization" shares the same root as "optimal", it is rare for the process of optimization to produce a truly optimal system. The optimized system will typically only be optimal in one application or for one audience. One might reduce the amount of time that a programme takes to perform some task at the price of making it consume more memory. In an application where memory space is at a premium, one might deliberately choose a slower algorithm in order to use less memory. Often there is no "one size fits all" design which works well in all cases, so engineers make trade-offs to optimize the attributes of greatest interest. Additionally, the effort required to make a piece of software completely optimal— incapable of any further improvement— is almost always more than is reasonable for the benefits that would be accrued; so the process of optimization may be halted before a completely optimal solution has been reached.

Fortunately, it is often the case that the greatest improvements come early in the process.

"Levels" of Optimization

Optimization can occur at a number of "levels":

- Design level
  At the highest level, the design may be optimized to make best use of the available resources. The implementation of this design will benefit from a good choice of efficient algorithms and the implementation of these algorithms will benefit from writing good quality code. The architectural design of a system overwhelmingly affects its performance. The choice of algorithm affects efficiency more than any other item of the design and, since the choice of algorithm usually is the first thing that must be decided, arguments against early or "premature optimization" may be hard to justify.
  In some cases, however, optimization relies on using more elaborate algorithms, making use of 'special cases' and special 'tricks' and performing complex trade-offs. A 'fully optimized' programme might be more difficult to comprehend and hence may contain more faults than unoptimized versions.
- Source code level
  Avoiding poor quality coding can also improve performance, by avoiding obvious 'slowdowns'. After that, however, some optimizations are possible that actually decrease maintainability. Some, but not all, optimizations can nowadays be performed by optimizing compilers.
- Compile level
  Use of an optimizing compiler tends to ensure that the executable programme is optimized at least as much as the compiler can predict.

- Assembly level

  At the lowest level, writing code using an assembly language, designed for a particular hardware platform can produce the most efficient and compact code if the programmer takes advantage of the full repertoire of machine instructions. Many operating systems used on embedded systems have been traditionally written in assembler code for this reason. Programmes (other than very small programmes) are seldom written from start to finish in assembly due to the time and cost involved. Most are complied down from a high level language to assembly and hand optimized from there. When efficiency and size are less important large parts may be written in a high-level language.

  With more modern optimizing compilers and the greater complexity of recent CPUs, it is more difficult to write code that is optimized better than the compiler itself generates, and few projects need resort to this 'ultimate' optimization step.

  However, a large amount of code written today is still compiled with the intent to run on the greatest percentage of machines possible. As a consequence, programmers and compilers don't always take advantage of the more efficient instructions provided by newer CPUs or quirks of older models. Additionally, assembly code tuned for a particular processor without using such instructions might still be suboptimal on a different processor, expecting a different tuning of the code.

- Run time

  Just-in-time compilers and Assembler programmers may be able to perform run time optimization exceeding the capability of static compilers by dynamically adjusting parameters according to the actual input or other factors.

Platform Dependent and Independent Optimizations

Code optimization can be also broadly categorized as platform-dependent and platform-independent techniques. While the latter ones are effective on most or all platforms, platform-dependent techniques use specific properties of one platform, or rely on parameters depending on the single platform or even on the single processor. Writing or producing different versions of the same code for different processors might therefore be needed. For instance, in the case of compile-level optimization, platform-independent techniques are generic techniques (such as loop unrolling, reduction in function calls, memory efficient routines, reduction in conditions, etc.), that impact most CPU architectures in a similar way. Generally, these serve to reduce the total Instruction path length required to complete the programme and/or reduce total memory usage during the process. On the other hand, platform-dependent techniques involve instruction scheduling, instruction-level parallelism, data-level parallelism, cache optimization techniques (i.e. parameters that differ among various platforms) and the optimal instruction scheduling might be different even on different processors of the same architecture.

Different Algorithms

Computational tasks can be performed in several different ways with varying efficiency. For example, consider the following C code snippet whose intention is to obtain the sum of all integers from 1 to N:

```
int i, sum = 0;
for (i = 1; i <= N; i++)
 sum += i;
printf ("sum: %d\n", sum);
```

This code can (assuming no arithmetic overflow) be rewritten using a mathematical formula like:

```
int sum = (N * (N+1)) / 2;
printf ("sum: %d\n", sum);
```

The optimization, sometimes performed automatically by an optimizing compiler, is to select a method (algorithm) that is more computationally efficient, while retaining the same functionality. See Algorithmic efficiency for a discussion of some of these techniques. However, a significant improvement in performance can often be achieved by removing extraneous functionality. Optimization is not always an obvious or intuitive process. In the example above, the 'optimized' version might actually be slower than the original version if N were sufficiently small and the particular hardware happens to be much faster at performing addition and looping operations than multiplication and bit-shifting.

Trade-Offs

Optimization will generally focus on improving just one or two aspects of performance: execution time, memory usage, disk space, bandwidth, power consumption or some other resource. This will usually require a trade-off - where one factor is optimized at the expense of others. For example, increasing the size of cache improves runtime performance, but also increases the memory consumption. Other common trade-offs include code clarity and conciseness.

There are instances where the programmer performing the optimization must decide to make the software better for some operations but at the cost of making other operations less efficient.

These trade-offs may sometimes be of a non-technical nature - such as when a competitor has published a benchmark result that must be beaten in order to improve commercial success but comes perhaps with the burden of making normal usage of the software less efficient. Such changes are sometimes jokingly referred to as *pessimizations*.

Bottlenecks

Optimization may include finding a bottleneck, a critical part of the code that is the primary consumer of the needed resource — sometimes known as a hot spot. Often, the Pareto principle is applied. i.e., 20% of the code is responsible for 80% of the results. In computer science, the Pareto principle can be applied to resource optimization by observing that 80% of the resources are typically used by 20% of the operations. In software engineering, it is often a better approximation that 90% of the execution time of a computer programme is spent executing 10% of the code (known as the 90/10 law in this context). More complex algorithms and data structures perform well with many items, while simple algorithms are more suitable for small amounts of data — the setup, initialization time, and constant factors of the more complex algorithm can outweigh the benefit. In some cases, adding more memory can help to make a programme run faster. For example, a filtering programme will commonly read each line and filter and output that line immediately. This only uses enough memory for one line, but performance is typically poor. Performance can be greatly improved by reading the entire file then writing the filtered result, though this uses much more memory. Caching the result is similarly effective, though also requiring larger memory use.

When to Optimize

Optimization can reduce readability and add code that is used only to improve the performance. This may complicate programmes or systems, making them harder to maintain and debug. As a result, optimization or performance tuning is often performed at the end of the development stage. Donald Knuth made the following two statements on optimization:

> "We should forget about small efficiencies, say about 97% of the time: premature optimization is the root of all evil"

(He also attributed the quote to Tony Hoare several years later, although this might have been an error as Hoare disclaims having coined the phrase.)

> "In established engineering disciplines a 12 % improvement, easily obtained, is never considered marginal and I believe the same viewpoint should prevail in software engineering"
>
> "Premature optimization" is a phrase used to describe a situation where a programmer lets performance considerations affect the design of a piece of code. This can result in a design that is not as clean as it could have been or code that is incorrect, because the code is complicated by the optimization and the programmer is distracted by optimizing.

An alternative approach is to design first, code from the design and then profile/benchmark the resulting code to see which parts should be optimized. A simple and elegant design is often easier to optimize at this stage, and profiling may reveal unexpected performance problems that would not have been addressed by premature optimization. In practice, it is often necessary to keep performance goals in mind when first designing software, but the programmer balances the goals of design and optimization.

Macros

Optimization during code development using macros takes on different forms in different languages. In some procedural languages, such as C and C++, macros are implemented using token substitution. Nowadays, inline functions can be used as a type safe alternative in many cases. In both cases, the inlined function body can then undergo further compile-time optimizations by the compiler, including constant folding, which may move some computations to compile time. In many functional programming languages macros are implemented using parse-time substitution of parse trees/abstract syntax trees, which it is claimed makes them safer to use. Since in many cases interpretation is used, that is one way to ensure that such computations are only performed at parse-time, and sometimes the only way. Lisp originated this style of macro, and such macros are often called "Lisp-like macros." A similar effect can be achieved by using Template metaprogramming in C++. In both cases, work is moved to compile-time. The difference between C macros on one side, and Lisp-like macros and C++ Template metaprogramming on the other side, is that the latter tools allow performing arbitrary computations at compile-time/parse-time, while expansion of C macros does not perform any computation, and relies on the optimizer ability to perform it. Additionally, C macros do not directly support recursion or iteration, so are not Turing complete. As with any optimization, however, it is often difficult to predict where such tools will have the most impact before a project is complete.

Automated and Manual Optimization

Optimization can be automated by compilers or performed by programmers. Gains are usually limited for local optimization, and larger for global optimizations. Usually, the most powerful optimization is to find a superior algorithm. Optimizing a whole system is usually undertaken by programmers because it is too complex for automated optimizers. In this situation, programmers or system administrators explicitly change code so that the overall system performs better. Although it can produce better efficiency, it is far more expensive than automated optimizations. Use a profiler (or performance analyzer) to find the sections of the programme that are taking the most resources — the *bottleneck*. Programmers sometimes believe they have a clear idea of where the bottleneck is, but intuition is frequently wrong. Optimizing an unimportant piece of code will typically do little to help the overall performance. When the bottleneck is localized, optimization usually starts with a rethinking of the algorithm used in the programme. More often than not, a particular algorithm can be specifically tailored to a particular problem, yielding better performance than a generic algorithm. For example, the task of sorting a huge list of items is usually done with a quicksort routine, which is one of the most efficient generic algorithms. But if some characteristic of the items is exploitable (for example, they are already arranged in some particular order), a different method can be used, or even a custom-made sort routine.

After the programmer is reasonably sure that the best algorithm is selected, code optimization can start. Loops can be unrolled (for lower loop overhead, although this can often lead to *lower* speed if it overloads the CPU cache), data types as small as possible can be used, integer arithmetic can be used instead of floating-point, and so on. Performance bottlenecks can be due to language limitations rather than algorithms or data structures used in the programme. Sometimes, a critical part of the programme can be re-written in a different programming language that gives more direct access to the underlying machine. For example, it is common for very high-level languages like Python to have modules written in C for greater speed. Programmes already written in C can have modules written in assembly. Programmes written in D can use the inline assembler.

Rewriting sections 'pays off' in these circumstances because of a general "rule of thumb" known as the 90/10 law, which states that 90% of the time is spent in 10% of the code, and only 10% of the time in the remaining 90% of the code. So, putting intellectual effort into optimizing just a small part of the programme can have a huge effect on the overall speed - if the correct part(s) can be located. Manual optimization sometimes has the side effect of undermining readability. Thus code optimizations should be carefully documented (preferably using in-line comments), and their effect on future development evaluated. The programme that performs an automated optimization is called an optimizer. Most optimizers are embedded in compilers and operate during compilation. Optimizers can often tailor the generated code to specific processors. Today, automated optimizations are almost exclusively limited to compiler optimization. However, because compiler optimizations are usually limited to a fixed set of rather general optimizations, there is considerable demand for optimizers which can accept descriptions of problem and language-specific optimizations, allowing an engineer to specify custom optimizations. Tools that accept descriptions of optimizations are called programme transformation systems and are beginning to be applied to real software systems such as C++. Some high-level languages (Eiffel, Esterel) optimize their programmes by using an intermediate language. Grid computing or distributed computing aims to optimize the whole system, by moving tasks from computers with high usage to computers with idle time.

Time Taken for Optimization

Sometimes, the time taken to undertake optimization in itself may be an issue. Optimizing existing code usually does not add new features, and worse, it might add new bugs in previously working code (as any change might). Because manually optimized code might sometimes have less 'readability' than unoptimized code, optimization might impact maintainability of it also. Optimization comes at a price and it is important to be sure that the investment is worthwhile. An automatic optimizer (or optimizing compiler, a programme that performs code optimization) may itself have to be optimized, either to further improve the efficiency of its target programmes or else speed up its own operation. A compilation performed with optimization 'turned on' usually takes longer, although this is usually only a problem when programmes are quite large. In particular, for just-in-time compilers the performance of the run time compile component, executing together with its target code, is the key to improving overall execution speed.

Famous Quotes

- *"The order in which the operations shall be performed in every particular case is a very interesting and curious question, on which our space does not permit us fully to enter. In almost every computation a great variety of arrangements for the succession of the processes is possible, and various considerations must influence the selection amongst them for the purposes of a Calculating Engine. One essential object is to choose that arrangement which shall tend to reduce to a minimum the time necessary for completing the calculation."* - Ada Byron's notes on the analytical engine 1842.
- *"More computing sins are committed in the name of efficiency (without necessarily achieving it) than for any other single reason - including blind stupidity."* - W.A. Wulf
- *"We should forget about small efficiencies, say about 97% of the time: premature optimization is the root of all evil. Yet we should not pass up our opportunities in that critical 3%.A good programmer will not be lulled into complacency by such reasoning, he will be wise to look carefully at the critical code; but only after that code has been identified"* - Donald Knuth
- *"Bottlenecks occur in surprising places, so don't try to second guess and put in a speed hack until you have proven that's where the bottleneck is."* - Rob Pike
- *"The First Rule of Programme Optimization: Don't do it. The Second Rule of Programme Optimization (for experts only!): Don't do it yet."* - Michael A. Jackson

REFERENCES

Frank Rubin published a criticism of Dijkstra's letter in the March 1987 CACM where it appeared under the title *'GOTO Considered Harmful' Considered Harmful.* Frank Rubin (March 1987). ""GOTO Considered Harmful" Considered Harmful" (PDF). *Communications of the ACM* 30 (3): 195–196.

Guy Lewis Steele, Jr. "Debunking the 'Expensive Procedure Call' Myth, or, Procedure Call Implementations Considered Harmful, or, Lambda: The Ultimate GOTO". MIT AI Lab. AI Lab Memo AIM-443. October 1977.

Knuth, Donald. *Structured Programming with go to Statements*, ACM Journal Computing Surveys, Vol 6, No. 4, Dec. 1974. p. 268.

Knuth, Donald: Structured Programming with Goto Statements. *Computing Surveys* 6:4 (1974), 261–301.

Kuketayev. "The Data Abstraction Penalty (DAP) Benchmark for Small Objects in Java.". http://www.adtmag.com/joop/article.aspx?id=4597. Retrieved 2008-03-17.

Springer Book High Level Synthesis From Algorithm to Digital Circuit ISBN 978-1-4020-8587-1

Surana P (2006) (PDF). *Meta-Compilation of Language Abstractions.*. ftp://lispnyc.org/meeting-assets/2007-02-13_pinku/SuranaThesis.pdf. Retrieved 2008-03-17.

4

Algorithm Trading and Computer Programme Profiling

ALGORITHMIC TRADING

In electronic financial markets, algorithmic trading or automated trading, also known as algo trading, black-box trading or robo trading, is the use of computer programmes for entering trading orders with the computer algorithm deciding on aspects of the order such as the timing, price, or quantity of the order, or in many cases initiating the order without human intervention. Algorithmic Trading is widely used by pension funds, mutual funds, and other buy side (investor driven) institutional traders, to divide large trades into several smaller trades in order to manage market impact, and risk. Sell side traders, such as market makers and some hedge funds, provide liquidity to the market, generating and executing orders automatically. A special class of algorithmic trading is "high-frequency trading" (HFT), in which computers make elaborate decisions to initiate orders based on information that is received electronically, before human traders are capable of processing the information they observe. This has resulted in a dramatic change of the market microstructure, particularly in the way liquidity is provided.

Algorithmic trading may be used in any investment strategy, including market making, inter-market spreading, arbitrage, or pure speculation (including trend following).

The investment decision and implementation may be augmented at any stage with algorithmic support or may operate completely automatically ("on auto-pilot"). A third of all EU and US stock trades in 2006 were driven by automatic programmes, or algorithms, according to Boston-based financial services industry research and consulting firm Aite Group. As of 2009, HFT firms account for 73% of all US equity trading volume.

In 2006 at the London Stock Exchange, over 40% of all orders were entered by algo traders, with 60% predicted for 2007. American markets and European markets generally have a higher proportion of algo trades than other markets, and estimates for 2008 range as high as an 80% proportion in some markets. Foreign exchange markets also have active algo trading (about 25% of orders in 2006). Futures and options markets are considered to be fairly easily integrated into algorithmic trading, with about 20% of options volume expected to be computer generated by 2010. Bond markets are moving toward more access to algorithmic traders. One of the main issues regarding HFT is the difficulty in determining just how profitable it is. A report released in August 2009 by the TABB Group, a financial services industry research firm, estimated that the 300 securities firms and hedge funds that specialize in this type of trading took in roughly US$21 billion in profits in 2008. Algorithmic and HFT have been the subject of much public debate since the U.S. Securities and Exchange Commission and the Commodity Futures Trading Commission implicated them in the May 6, 2010 Flash Crash, when the Dow Jones Industrial Average suffered its largest intraday point loss ever to that date, though prices quickly recovered.

History

Computerization of the order flow in financial markets began in the early 1970s with some landmarks being the introduction of the New York Stock Exchange's "designated order turnaround" system (DOT, and later SuperDOT) which routed orders electronically to the proper trading post to be executed manually, and the "opening automated reporting system" (OARS) which aided the specialist in determining the market clearing opening price (SOR; Smart Order Routing). Programme trading is defined by the New York Stock Exchange as an order to buy or sell 15 or more stocks valued at over US$1 million total. In practice this means that all programme trades are entered with the aid of a computer. In the 1980s programme trading became widely used in trading between the S&P500 equity and futures markets. In stock index arbitrage a trader buys (or sells) a stock index futures contract such as the S&P 500 futures and sells (or buys) a portfolio of up to 500 stocks (can be a much smaller representative subset) at the NYSE matched against the futures trade. The programme trade at the NYSE would be pre-programmed into a computer to enter the order automatically into the NYSE's electronic order routing system at a time when the futures price and the stock index were far enough apart to make a profit.

At about the same time portfolio insurance was designed to create a synthetic put option on a stock portfolio by dynamically trading stock index futures according to a computer model based on the Black-Scholes option pricing model. Both strategies, often simply lumped together as "programme trading", were blamed by many people (for example by the Brady report) for exacerbating or even starting the 1987 stock market crash. Yet the impact of computer driven trading on stock market crashes is unclear and widely discussed in the academic community. Financial markets with fully electronic execution and similar electronic communication networks developed in the late 1980s and 1990s. In the U.S., decimalization, which changed the minimum tick size from 1/16 of a dollar (US$0.0625) to US$0.01 per share, may have encouraged algorithmic trading as it changed the market microstructure by permitting smaller differences between the bid and offer prices, decreasing the market-makers' trading advantage, thus increasing market liquidity.

This increased market liquidity led to institutional traders splitting up orders according to computer algorithms in order to execute their orders at a better average price. These average price benchmarks are measured and calculated by computers by applying the time weighted (i.e. unweighted) average price TWAP or more usually by the volume weighted average price VWAP. As more electronic markets opened, other algorithmic trading strategies were introduced. These strategies are more easily implemented by computers because machines can react more rapidly to temporary mispricing and examine prices from several markets simultaneously. For example Stealth (developed by the *Deutsche Bank*), Sniper and Guerilla (developed by *Credit Suisse*), arbitrage, statistical arbitrage, trend following, and mean reversion. This type of trading is what is driving the new demand for Low Latency Proximity Hosting and Global Exchange Connectivity. It is imperative to understand what is latency when putting together a strategy for electronic trading. Latency refers to the delay between the transmission of information from a source and the reception of the information at a destination. Latency has as a lower bound the speed of light; this corresponds to a few microseconds per 1,000 kilometers of optical fibre. Any signal regenerating or routing equipment will introduce greater latency than this speed-of-light baseline.

Strategies

Trend Following

Trend following is an investment strategy that tries to take advantage of long-term moves that seem to play out in various markets. The system aims to work on the market trend mechanism and take benefit from both sides of the market enjoying the profits from the *ups* and *downs* of the stock or futures markets. Traders who use this approach can use current market price calculation, moving averages and channel breakouts to determine the general direction of the market and to generate trade signals. Traders who subscribe to a trend following strategy do not aim to forecast or predict specific price levels; they simply jump on the trend and ride it.

Pair Trading

The pairs trade or pair trading is a market neutral trading strategy enabling traders to profit from virtually any market conditions: uptrend, downtrend, or sidewise movement. This trading strategy is categorized as a statistical arbitrage and convergence trading strategy.

Delta Neutral Strategies

In finance, delta neutral describes a portfolio of related financial securities, in which the portfolio value remains unchanged due to small changes in the value of the underlying security.

Such a portfolio typically contains options and their corresponding underlying securities such that positive and negative delta components offset, resulting in the portfolio's value being relatively insensitive to changes in the value of the underlying security.

Arbitrage

In economics and finance, arbitrage is the practice of taking advantage of a price difference between two or more markets: striking a combination of matching deals that capitalize upon the imbalance, the profit being the difference between the market prices. When used by academics, an arbitrage is a transaction that involves no negative cash flow at any probabilistic or temporal state and a positive cash flow in at least one state; in simple terms, it is the possibility of a risk-free profit at zero cost.

Conditions for Arbitrage

Arbitrage is possible when one of three conditions is met:

1. The same asset does not trade at the same price on all markets (the "law of one price").
2. Two assets with identical cash flows do not trade at the same price.
3. An asset with a known price in the future does not today trade at its future price discounted at the risk-free interest rate (or, the asset does not have negligible costs of storage; as such, for example, this condition holds for grain but not for securities).

Arbitrage is not simply the act of buying a product in one market and selling it in another for a higher price at some later time. The transactions must occur *simultaneously* to avoid exposure to market risk, or the risk that prices may change on one market before both transactions are complete. In practical terms, this is generally only possible with securities and financial products which can be traded electronically, and even then, when each leg of the trade is executed the prices in the market may have moved. Missing one of the legs of the trade (and subsequently having to trade it soon after at a worse price) is called 'execution risk' or more specifically 'leg risk'. In the simplest example, any good sold in one market should sell for the same price in another. Traders may, for example, find that the price of wheat is lower in agricultural regions than in cities, purchase the good, and transport it to another region to sell at a higher price. This type of price arbitrage is the most common, but this simple example ignores the cost of transport, storage, risk, and other factors. "True" arbitrage requires that there be no market risk involved. Where securities are traded on more than one exchange, arbitrage occurs by simultaneously buying in one and selling on the other.

Mean Reversion

Mean reversion is a mathematical methodology sometimes used for stock investing, but it can be applied to other processes. In general terms the idea is that both a stock's high and low prices are temporary, and that a stock's price will tend to have an average price over time. Mean reversion involves first identifying the trading range for a stock, and then computing the average price using analytical techniques as it relates to assets, earnings, etc. When the current market price is less than the average price, the stock is considered attractive for purchase, with the expectation that the price will rise. When the current market price is above the average price, the market price is expected to fall. In other words, deviations from the average price are expected to revert to the average. The Standard deviation of the most recent prices (e.g., the last 20) is often used as a buy or sell indicator. Stock reporting services (such as Yahoo! Finance, MS Investor, Morningstar, etc.), commonly offer moving averages for periods such as 50 and 100 days. While reporting services provide the averages, identifying the high and low prices for the study period is still necessary. Mean reversion has the appearance of a more scientific method of choosing stock buy and sell points than charting, because precise numerical values are derived from historical data to identify the buy/sell values, rather than trying to interpret price movements using charts (charting, also known as technical analysis).

Scalping

Scalping (trading) is a method of arbitrage of small price gaps created by the bid-ask spread. Scalpers attempt to act like traditional market makers or specialists. To *make the spread* means to buy at the Bid price and sell at the Ask price, to gain the bid/ask difference. This procedure allows for profit even when the bid and ask do not move at all, as long as there are traders who are willing to take market prices. It normally involves establishing and liquidating a position quickly, usually within minutes or even seconds. The role of a scalper is actually the role of market makers or specialists who are to maintain the liquidity and order flow of a product of a market. A market maker is basically a specialized scalper. The volume a market maker trades are many times more than the average individual scalpers. A market maker has a sophisticated trading system to monitor trading activity. However, a market maker is bound by strict exchange rules while the individual trader is not. For instance, NASDAQ requires each market maker to post at least one bid and one ask at some price level, so as to maintain a two-sided market for each stock represented.

Transaction Cost Reduction

Most strategies referred to as Algorithmic Trading (as well as algorithmic liquidity seeking) fall into the cost-reduction category. Large orders are broken down into several smaller orders and entered into the market over time. This basic strategy is called "iceberging". The success of this strategy may be measured by the average purchase price against the VWAP for the market over that time period. One algorithm designed to find hidden orders or icebergs is called "Stealth". Most of these strategies were first documented in 'Optimal Trading Strategies' by Robert Kissell.

Strategies that Only Pertain to Dark Pools

Recently, HFT, which comprises a broad set of buy-side as well as market making sell side traders, has become more prominent and controversial. These algorithms or techniques are commonly given names such as "Stealth" (developed by the Deutsche Bank), "Iceberg", "Dagger", "Guerrilla", "Sniper", "BASOR" (developed by Quod Financial) and "Sniffer". Yet are at their core quite simple mathematical constructs. Dark pools are alternative electronic stock exchanges where trading takes place anonymously, with most orders hidden or "iceberged." Gamers or "sharks" sniff out large orders by "pinging" small market orders to buy and sell. When several small orders are filled the sharks may have discovered the presence of a large iceberged order. "Now it's an arms race," said Andrew Lo, director of the Massachusetts Institute of Technology's Laboratory for Financial Engineering. "Everyone is building more sophisticated algorithms, and the more competition exists, the smaller the profits." One of the unintended adverse effects of algorithmic trading, has been the dramatic increase in the volume of trade allocations and settlements, as well as the transaction settlement costs associated with them. Since 2004, there have been a number of technological advances and service providers by individuals like Scott Kurland, who have built solutions for aggregating trades executed across algorithms, in order to counter these rising settlement costs.

High-Frequency Trading

In the U.S., high-frequency trading (HFT) firms represent 2% of the approximately 20,000 firms operating today, but account for 73% of all equity trading volume. As of the first quarter in 2009, total assets under management for hedge funds with HFT strategies were US$141 billion, down about 21% from their high. The HFT strategy was first made successful by Renaissance Technologies. High-frequency funds started to become especially popular in 2007 and 2008. Many HFT firms are market makers and provide liquidity to the market which has lowered volatility and helped narrow Bid-offer spreads making trading and investing cheaper for other market participants. HFT has been a subject of intense public focus since the U.S. Securities and Exchange Commission and the Commodity Futures Trading Commission implicated both algorithmic and HFT in the May 6, 2010 Flash Crash. High-frequency trading is quantitative trading that is characterized by short portfolio holding periods. There are four key categories of HFT strategies: market-making based on order flow, market-making based on tick data information, event arbitrage and statistical arbitrage. All portfolio-allocation decisions are made by computerized quantitative models. The success of HFT strategies is largely driven by their ability to simultaneously process volumes of information, something ordinary human traders cannot do.

Market Making

Market making is a set of HFT strategies that involves placing a limit order to sell (or offer) above the current market price or a buy limit order (or bid) below the current price in order to benefit from the bid-ask spread. Automated Trading Desk, which was bought by Citigroup in July 2007, has been an active market maker, accounting for about 6% of total volume on both NASDAQ and the New York Stock Exchange.

Statistical Arbitrage

Another set of HFT strategies is classical arbitrage strategy might involve several securities such as covered interest rate parity in the foreign exchange market which gives a relation between the prices of a domestic bond, a bond denominated in a foreign currency, the spot price of the currency, and the price of a forward contract on the currency. If the market prices are sufficiently different from those implied in the model to cover transactions cost then four transactions can be made to guarantee a risk-free profit. HFT allows similar arbitrages using models of greater complexity involving many more than 4 securities. The TABB Group estimates that annual aggregate profits of low latency arbitrage strategies currently exceed US$21 billion. A wide range of statistical arbitrage strategies have been developed whereby trading decisions are made on the basis of deviations from statistically significant relationships. Like market-making strategies, statistical arbitrage can be applied in all asset classes.

Event Arbitrage

A subset of risk, merger, convertible, or distressed securities arbitrage that counts on a specific event, such as a contract signing, regulatory approval, judicial decision, etc., to change the price or rate relationship of two or more financial instruments and permit the arbitrageur to earn a profit. Merger arbitrage also called risk arbitrage would be an example of this. Merger arbitrage generally consists of buying the stock of a company that is the target of a takeover while shorting the stock of the acquiring company. Usually the market price of the target company is less than the price offered by the acquiring company. The spread between these two prices depends mainly on the probability and the timing of the takeover being completed as well as the prevailing level of interest rates. The bet in a merger arbitrage is that such a spread will eventually be zero, if and when the takeover is completed. The risk is that the deal "breaks" and the spread massively widens.

Low-Latency Trading

HFT is often confused with low-latency trading that uses computers that execute trades within milliseconds, or "with extremely low latency" in the jargon of the trade. Low-latency trading is highly dependent on ultra-low latency networks. They profit by providing information, such as competing bids and offers, to their algorithms microseconds faster than their competitors. The revolutionary advance in speed has led to the need for firms to have a real-time, colocated trading platform in order to benefit from implementing high-frequency strategies. Strategies are constantly altered to reflect the subtle changes in the market as well as to combat the threat of the strategy being reverse engineered by competitors. There is also a very strong pressure to continuously add features or improvements to a particular algorithm, such as client specific modifications and various performance enhancing changes (regarding benchmark trading performance, cost reduction for the trading firm or a range of other implementations). This is due to the evolutionary nature of algorithmic trading strategies - they must be able to adapt and trade intelligently, regardless of market conditions, which involves being flexible enough to withstand a vast array of market scenarios. As a result, a significant proportion of net revenue from firms is spent on the R&D of these autonomous trading systems.

Strategy Implementation

Most of the algorithmic strategies are implemented using modern programming languages, although some still implement strategies designed in spreadsheets. Basic models can rely on as little as a linear regression, while more complex game-theoretic and pattern recognition or predictive models can also be used to initiate trading. Neural networks and genetic programming have been used to create these models.

Issues and Developments

Algorithmic trading has been shown to substantially improve market liquidity among other benefits. However, improvements in productivity brought by algorithmic trading have been opposed by human brokers and traders facing stiff competition from computers.

Concerns

"The downside with these systems is their black boxness," Mr. Williams said. "Traders have intuitive senses of how the world works. But with these systems you pour in a bunch of numbers, and something comes out the other end, and it's not always intuitive or clear why the black box latched onto certain data or relationships." "The Financial Services Authority has been keeping a watchful eye on the development of black box trading. In its annual report the regulator remarked on the great benefits of efficiency that new technology is bringing to the market. But it also pointed out that 'greater reliance on sophisticated technology and modelling brings with it a greater risk that systems failure can result in business interruption'." UK Treasury minister Lord Myners has warned that companies could become the "playthings" of speculators because of automatic high-frequency trading. Lord Myners said the process risked destroying the relationship between an investor and a company. Other issues include the technical problem of latency or the delay in getting quotes to traders, security and the possibility of a complete system breakdown leading to a market crash. "Goldman spends tens of millions of dollars on this stuff. They have more people working in their technology area than people on the trading desk...The nature of the markets has changed dramatically." Algorithmic and HTF were implicated in the May 6, 2010 Flash Crash, when the Dow Jones Industrial Average plunged about 600 points only to recover those losses within minutes. At the time, it was the second largest point swing, 1,010.14 points, and the biggest one-day point decline, 998.5 points, on an intraday basis in Dow Jones Industrial Average history.

Recent Developments

Financial market news is now being formatted by firms such as Need To Know News, Thomson Reuters, Dow Jones, and Bloomberg, to be read and traded on via algorithms. "Computers are now being used to generate news stories about company earnings results or economic statistics as they are released. And this almost instantaneous information forms a direct feed into other computers which trade on the news." The algorithms do not simply trade on simple news stories but also interpret more difficult to understand news. Some firms are also attempting to automatically assign *sentiment* (deciding if the news is good or bad) to news stories so that automated trading can work directly on the news story. "Increasingly, people are looking at all forms of news and building their own indicators around it in a semi-structured way," as they constantly seek out new trading advantages said Rob Passarella, global director of strategy at Dow Jones Enterprise Media Group. His firm provides both a low latency news feed and news analytics for traders.

Passarella also pointed to new academic research being conducted on the degree to which frequent Google searches on various stocks can serve as trading indicators, the potential impact of various phrases and words that may appear in Securities and Exchange Commission statements and the latest wave of online communities devoted to stock trading topics. "Markets are by their very nature conversations, having grown out of coffee houses and taverns", he said.

So the way conversations get created in a digital society will be used to convert news into trades, as well, Passarella said. "There is a real interest in moving the process of interpreting news from the humans to the machines" says Kirsti Suutari, global business manager of algorithmic trading at Reuters. "More of our customers are finding ways to use news content to make money."

An example of the importance of news reporting speed to algorithmic traders was an advertising campaign by Dow Jones (appearances included page W15 of the Wall Street Journal, on March 1, 2008) claiming that their service had beaten other news services by 2 seconds in reporting an interest rate cut by the Bank of England. In July 2007, Citigroup, which had already developed its own trading algorithms, paid $680 million for Automated Trading Desk, a 19-year-old firm that trades about 200 million shares a day. Citigroup had previously bought Lava Trading and OnTrade Inc.

Technical Design

The technical designs of such systems are not standardized. Conceptually, the design can be divided into logical units:

1. The data stream unit (the part of the systems that receives data (e.g. quotes, news) from external sources).
2. The decision or strategy unit
3. The execution unit.

With the wide use of social networks, some systems implement scanning or screening technologies to read posts of users extracting human sentiment and influence the trading strategies.

Effects

Though its development may have been prompted by decreasing trade sizes caused by decimalization, algorithmic trading has reduced trade sizes further. Jobs once done by human traders are being switched to computers. The speeds of computer connections, measured in milliseconds and even microseconds, have become very important. More fully automated markets such as NASDAQ, Direct Edge and BATS, in the US, have gained market share from less automated markets such as the NYSE. Economies of scale in electronic trading have contributed to lowering commissions and trade processing fees, and contributed to international mergers and consolidation of financial exchanges. Competition is developing among exchanges for the fastest processing times for completing trades. For example, in June 2007, the London Stock Exchange launched a new system called TradElect that promises an average 10 millisecond turnaround time from placing an order to final confirmation and can process 3,000 orders per second. Since then, competitive exchanges have continued to reduce latency with turnaround times of 3 milliseconds available.

This is of great importance to high-frequency traders because they have to attempt to pinpoint the consistent and probable performance ranges of given financial instruments. These professionals are often dealing in versions of stock index funds like the E-mini S&Ps because they seek consistency and risk-mitigation along with top performance. They must filter market data to work into their software programming so that there is the lowest latency and highest liquidity at the time for placing stop-losses and/or taking profits. With high volatility in these markets, this becomes a complex and potentially nerve-wracking endeavor, where a small mistake can lead to a large loss. Absolute frequency data play into the development of the trader's pre-programmed instructions. Spending on computers and software in the financial industry increased to $26.4 billion in 2005.

Communication Standards

Algorithmic trades require communicating considerably more parameters than traditional market and limit orders. A trader on one end (the "buy side") must enable their trading system (often called an "Order Management System" or "Execution Management System") to understand a constantly proliferating flow of new algorithmic order types. The R&D and other costs to construct complex new algorithmic orders types, along with the execution infrastructure, and marketing costs to distribute them, are fairly substantial. What was needed was a way that marketers (the "sell side") could express algo orders electronically such that buy-side traders could just drop the new order types into their system and be ready to trade them without constant coding custom new order entry screens each time. FIX Protocol LTD http://www.fixprotocol.org is a trade association that publishes free, open standards in the securities trading area. The FIX language was originally created by Fidelity Investments, and the association Members include virtually all large and many midsized and smaller broker dealers, money center banks, institutional investors, mutual funds, etc. This institution dominates standard setting in the pretrade and trade areas of security transactions. In 2006-2007 several members got together and published a draft XML standard for expressing algorithmic order types. The standard is called FIX Algorithmic Trading Definition Language (FIXatdl). The first version of this standard, 1.0 was not widely adopted due to limitations in the specification, but the second version, 1.1 (released in March 2010) is expected to achieve broad adoption and in the process dramatically reduce time-to-market and costs associated with distributing new algorithms.

PROFILING

In software engineering, programme profiling, software profiling or simply profiling, a form of dynamic programme analysis (as opposed to static code analysis), is the investigation of a program's behaviour using information gathered as the programme executes. The usual purpose of this analysis is to determine which sections of a programme to optimize - to increase its overall speed, decrease its memory requirement or sometimes both.

- A (code) profiler is a performance analysis tool that, most commonly, measures only the frequency and duration of function calls, but there are other specific types of profilers (e.g. memory profilers) in addition to more comprehensive profilers, capable of gathering extensive performance data.
- An instruction set simulator which is also — by necessity — a profiler, can measure the totality of a program's behaviour from invocation to termination.

Gathering Programme Events

Profilers use a wide variety of techniques to collect data, including hardware interrupts, code instrumentation, instruction set simulation, operating system hooks, and performance counters. The usage of profilers is 'called out' in the performance engineering process.

Use of Profilers

Programme analysis tools are extremely important for understanding programme behaviour. Computer architects need such tools to evaluate how well programmes will perform on new architectures. Software writers need tools to analyze their programmes and identify critical sections of code. Compiler writers often use such tools to find out how well their instruction scheduling or branch prediction algorithm is performing... (ATOM, PLDI, '94)

The output of a profiler may be:-

- A statistical *summary* of the events observed (a profile)
  Summary profile information is often shown annotated against the source code statements where the events occur, so the size of measurement data is linear to the code size of the programme.
- A stream of recorded events (a trace)
  For sequential programmes, a summary profile is usually sufficient, but performance problems in parallel programmes (waiting for messages or synchronization issues) often depend on the time relationship of events, thus requiring a full trace to get an understanding of what is happening.
  The size of a (full) trace is linear to the program's instruction path length, making it somewhat impractical. A trace may therefore be initiated at one point in a programme and terminated at another point to limit the output.
- An ongoing interaction with the hypervisor (continuous or periodic monitoring via on-screen display for instance)

This provides the opportunity to switch a trace on or off at any desired point during execution in addition to viewing on-going metrics about the (still executing) programme. It also provides the opportunity to suspend asynchronous processes at critical points to examine interactions with other parallel processes in more detail.

History

Performance analysis tools existed on IBM/360 and IBM/370 platforms from the early 1970s, usually based on timer interrupts which recorded the Programme status word (PSW) at set timer intervals to detect "hot spots" in executing code. This was an early example of sampling. In early 1974, Instruction Set Simulators permitted full trace and other performance monitoring features. Profiler-driven programme analysis on Unix dates back to at least 1979, when Unix systems included a basic tool "prof" that listed each function and how much of programme execution time it used. In 1982, gprof extended the concept to a complete call graph analysis. In 1994, Amitabh Srivastava and Alan Eustace of Digital Equipment Corporation published a paper describing ATOM. ATOM is a platform for converting a programme into its own profiler. That is, at compile time, it inserts code into the programme to be analyzed. That inserted code outputs analysis data. This technique - modifying a programme to analyze itself - is known as "instrumentation". In 2004, both the gprof and ATOM papers appeared on the list of the 50 most influential PLDI papers of all time.

Profiler Types Based on Output

Flat Profiler

Flat profilers compute the average call times, from the calls, and do not break down the call times based on the callee or the context.

Call-Graph Profiler

Call graph profilers show the call times, and frequencies of the functions, and also the call-chains involved based on the callee. However context is not preserved.

Methods of Data Gathering

Event-Based Profilers

The programming languages listed here have event-based profilers:

- Java: the JVMTI (JVM Tools Interface) API, formerly JVMPI (JVM Profiling Interface), provides hooks to profilers, for trapping events like calls, class-load, unload, thread enter leave.
- .NET: Can attach a profiling agent as a COM server to the CLR. Like Java, the runtime then provides various callbacks into the agent, for trapping events like method JIT / enter / leave, object creation, etc. Particularly powerful in that the profiling agent can rewrite the target application's bytecode in arbitrary ways.
- Python: Python profiling includes the profile module, hotshot (which is call-graph based), and using the 'sys.setprofile' function to trap events like c_{call,return,exception}, python_{call,return, exception}.
- Ruby: Ruby also uses a similar interface like Python for profiling. Flat-profiler in profile.rb, module, and ruby-prof a C-extension are present.

Statistical Profilers

Some profilers operate by sampling. A sampling profiler probes the target program's programme counter at regular intervals using operating system interrupts. Sampling profiles are typically less numerically accurate and specific, but allow the target programme to run at near full speed.

The resulting data are not exact, but a statistical approximation. *The actual amount of error is usually more than one sampling period. In fact, if a value is n times the sampling period, the expected error in it is the square-root of n sampling periods.* In practice, sampling profilers can often provide a more accurate picture of the target program's execution than other approaches, as they are not as intrusive to the target programme, and thus don't have as many side effects (such as on memory caches or instruction decoding pipelines). Also since they don't affect the execution speed as much, they can detect issues that would otherwise be hidden. They are also relatively immune to over-evaluating the cost of small, frequently called routines or 'tight' loops. They can show the relative amount of time spent in user mode versus interruptible kernel mode such as system call processing. Still, kernel code to handle the interrupts entails a minor loss of CPU cycles, diverted cache usage, and is unable to distinguish the various tasks occurring in uninterruptible kernel code (microsecond-range activity). Dedicated hardware can go beyond this: some recent MIPS processors JTAG interface have a PCSAMPLE register, which samples the programme counter in a truly undetectable manner. Some of the most commonly used statistical profilers are AMD CodeAnalyst, Apple Inc. Shark, gprof, Intel VTune and Parallel Amplifier (part of Intel Parallel Studio).

Instrumenting Profilers

Some profilers instrument the target programme with additional instructions to collect the required information. Instrumenting the programme can cause changes in the performance of the programme, potentially causing inaccurate results and heisenbugs. Instrumenting will always have some impact on the programme execution, typically always slowing it. However, instrumentation can be very specific and be carefully controlled to have a minimal impact. The impact on a particular programme depends on the placement of instrumentation points and the mechanism used to capture the trace. Hardware support for trace capture means that on some targets, instrumentation can be on just one machine instruction. The impact of instrumentation can often be deducted (i.e. eliminated by subtraction) from the results. gprof is an example of a profiler that uses both instrumentation and sampling. Instrumentation is used to gather caller information and the actual timing values are obtained by statistical sampling.

Instrumentation

- Manual: Performed by the programmer, e.g. by adding instructions to explicitly calculate runtimes, simply count events or calls to measurement APIs such as the Application Response Measurement standard.
- Automatic source level: instrumentation added to the source code by an automatic tool according to an instrumentation policy.
- Compiler assisted: Example: "gcc -pg ..." for gprof, "quantify g++ ..." for Quantify
- Binary translation: The tool adds instrumentation to a compiled binary. Example: ATOM
- Runtime instrumentation: Directly before execution the code is instrumented. The programme run is fully supervised and controlled by the tool. Examples: Pin, Valgrind
- Runtime injection: More lightweight than runtime instrumentation. Code is modified at runtime to have jumps to helper functions. Example: DynInst

Interpreter Instrumentation

- Interpreter debug options can enable the collection of performance metrics as the interpreter encounters each target statement. A bytecode, control table or JIT interpreters are three examples that usually have complete control over execution of the target code, thus enabling extremely comprehensive data collection opportunities.

Hypervisor/Simulator

- Hypervisor: Data are collected by running the (usually) unmodified programme under a hypervisor. Example: SIMMON
- Simulator and Hypervisor: Data collected interactively and selectively by running the unmodified programme under an Instruction Set Simulator. Examples: SIMON and OLIVER.

REFERENCES

Aldridge, Irene (2009), *High-Frequency Trading: A Practical Guide to Algorithmic Strategies and Trading Systems. Wiley & Sons* (Amazon.com), http://www.amazon.com/reader/0470563761?_encoding=UTF8&ref_=sib_dp_pt

Artificial intelligence applied heavily to picking stocks by Charles Duhigg, November 23, 2006

Atom: A system for building customized programme analysis tools, Amitabh Srivastava and Alan Eustace, 1994 (download)

Bowley, Graham (1 Oct 2010). "Lone $4.1 Billion Sale Led to 'Flash Crash' in May". The New York Times.

Cracking The Street's New Math, Algorithmic trades are sweeping the stock market.

Dunlavey, "Performance tuning with instruction-level cost derived from call-stack sampling", ACM SIGPLAN Notices 42, 8 (August, 2007), pp. 4–8.

Dunlavey, "Performance Tuning: Slugging It Out!", Dr. Dobb's Journal, Vol 18, #12, November 1993, pp 18–26.

Geoffrey Rogow, Rise of the (Market) Machines, *The Wall Street Journal*, June 19, 2009

Goldfarb, Zachary (1 Oct 2010). "Report examines May's 'flash crash,' expresses concern over high-speed trading". Washington Post.

Lauricella, Tom (2 Oct 2010). "How a Trading Algorithm Went Awry". The Wall Street Journal.

Lauricella, Tom, and McKay, Peter A. "Dow Takes a Harrowing 1,010.14-Point Trip," Online Wall Street Journal, May 7, 2010. Retrieved May 9, 2010

Looking for options Derivatives drive the battle of the exchanges, April 15, 2007, Economist.com

Mehta, Nina (1 Oct 2010). "Automatic Futures Trade Drove May Stock Crash, Report Says". Bloomberg.

Opalesque (4 August 2009). "Opalesque Exclusive: High-frequency trading under the microscope".

Popper, Nathaniel (1 Oct 2010). "$4.1-billion trade set off Wall Street 'flash crash,' report finds". Los Angeles Times.

Preis, T.; Paul, W.; Schneider, J. J. (2008), "Fluctuation patterns in high-frequency financial asset returns", *EPL (Europhysics Letters)* 82 (6): 68005,

Rob Curren, Watch Out for Sharks in Dark Pools, The Wall Street Journal, August 19, 2008, p. c5. Available at WSJ Blogs retrieved August 19, 2008

Rob Iati, The Real Story of Trading Software Espionage, *AdvancedTrading.com*, July 10, 2009

Spicer, Jonathan (1 Oct 2010). "Single U.S. trade helped spark May's flash crash". Reuters.

Spicer, Jonathan (15 Oct 2010). "Special report: Globally, the flash crash is no flash in the pan". Reuters.

Wilmott, Paul (July 29, 2009). "Hurrying into the Next Panic". *New York Times*: p. A19.

Younglai, Rachelle (5 Oct 2010). "U.S. probes computer algorithms after "flash crash"".

5

Towards Understanding the Theory of Computation and Partial Function

THEORY OF COMPUTATION

In theoretical computer science, the theory of computation is the branch that deals with whether and how efficiently problems can be solved on a model of computation, using an algorithm. The field is divided into three major branches: automata theory, computability theory and computational complexity theory. In order to perform a rigorous study of computation, computer scientists work with a mathematical abstraction of computers called a model of computation. There are several models in use, but the most commonly examined is the Turing machine. Computer scientists study the Turing machine because it is simple to formulate, can be analyzed and used to prove results, and because it represents what many consider the most powerful possible "reasonable" model of computation. It might seem that the potentially infinite memory capacity is an unrealizable attribute, but any decidable problem solved by a Turing machine will always require only a finite amount of memory. So in principle, any problem that can be solved (decided) by a Turing machine can be solved by a computer that has a bounded amount of memory.

History

The theory of computation can be considered the creation

of models of all kinds in the field of computer science. Therefore mathematics and logic are used. In the last century it became an independent academic discipline and was separated from mathematics.

Some pioneers of the theory of computation were Alonzo Church, Alan Turing, Stephen Kleene, John von Neumann, Claude Shannon, and Noam Chomsky.

Branches

Computability Theory

Computability theory deals primarily with the question of the extent to which a problem is solvable on a computer. The statement that the halting problem cannot be solved by a Turing machine is one of the most important results in computability theory, as it is an example of a concrete problem that is both easy to formulate and impossible to solve using a Turing machine. Much of computability theory builds on the halting problem result. Another important step in computability theory was Rice's theorem, which states that for all non-trivial properties of partial functions, it is undecidable whether a Turing machine computes a partial function with that property. Computability theory is closely related to the branch of mathematical logic called recursion theory, which removes the restriction of studying only models of computation which are reducible to the Turing model. Many mathematicians and computational theorists who study recursion theory will refer to it as computability theory.

Computational Complexity Theory

Complexity theory considers not only whether a problem can be solved at all on a computer, but also how efficiently the problem can be solved. Two major aspects are considered: time complexity and space complexity, which are respectively how many steps does it take to perform a computation, and how much memory is required to perform that computation. In order to analyze how much time and space a given algorithm requires, computer scientists express the time or space required to solve the problem as a function of the size of the input problem. For example, finding a particular number in a long list of numbers becomes harder as the list of numbers grows larger. If we say there are n numbers in the list, then if the list is not sorted or indexed in any way we may have to look at every number in order to find the number we're seeking. We thus say that in order to solve this problem, the computer needs to perform a number of steps that grows linearly in the size of the problem. To simplify this problem, computer scientists have adopted Big O notation, which allows functions to be compared in a way that ensures that particular aspects of a machine's construction do not need to be considered, but rather only the asymptotic behaviour as problems become large. So in our previous example we might say that the problem requires $O(n)$ steps to solve. Perhaps the most important open problem in all of computer science is the question of whether a certain broad class of problems denoted NP can be solved efficiently. This is discussed further at Complexity classes P and NP.

Models of Computation

Aside from a Turing machine, other equivalent models of computation are in use.

Lambda Calculus

A computation consists of an initial lambda expression (or two if you want to separate the function and its input) plus a finite sequence of lambda terms, each deduced from the preceding term by one application of Beta reduction.

Combinatory Logic

Combinatory Logic is a concept which has many similarities to ë-calculus, but also important differences exist (e.g. fixed point combinator Y has normal form in combinatory logic but not in ë-calculus). Combinatory logic was developed with great ambitions: understanding the nature of paradoxes, making foundations of mathematics more economic (conceptually), eliminating the notion of variables (thus clarifying their role in mathematics).

Mu-recursive Functions

Mu-recursive Functions (a) computation consists of a mu-recursive function, *i.e.* its defining sequence, any input value(s) and a sequence of recursive functions appearing in the defining sequence with inputs and outputs. Thus, if in the defining sequence of a recursive function $f(x)$ the functions $g(x)$ and $h(x,y)$ appear, then terms of the form 'g(5)=7' or 'h(3,2)=10' might appear. Each entry in this sequence needs to be an application of a basic function or follow from the entries above by using composition, primitive recursion or mu recursion. For instance if $f(x) = h(x,g(x))$, then for 'f(5)=3' to appear, terms like 'g(5)=6' and 'h(5,6)=3' must occur above. The computation terminates only if the final term gives the value of the recursive function applied to the inputs.

Markov Algorithm

A string rewriting system that uses grammar-like rules to operate on strings of symbols.

Register Machine

Register machine is a theoretically interesting idealization of a computer. There are several variants. In most of them, each register can hold a natural number (of unlimited size), and the instructions are simple (and few in number), e.g. only decrementation (combined with conditional jump) and incrementation exist (and halting). The lack of the infinite (or dynamically growing) external store can be understood by replacing its role with Gödel numbering techniques: the fact that each register holds a natural number allows the possibility of representing a complicated thing (e.g. a sequence, or a matrix etc.) by an appropriate huge natural number — unambiguity of both representation and interpretation can be established by number theoretical foundations of these techniques.

P2 2

Like Turing machines, P2 2 uses an infinite tape of symbols (without random access), and a rather minimalistic set of instructions. But these instructions are very different, thus, unlike Turing machines, P2 2 does not need to maintain a distinct state, because all "memory-like" functionality can be provided only by the tape. Instead of rewriting the current symbol, it can perform a modular arithmetic incrementation on it. P2 2 has also a pair of instructions for a cycle, inspecting the blank symbol.

Despite its minimalistic nature, it has become the parental formal language of an implemented and (for entertainment) used programming language called Brainfuck. In addition to the general computational models, some simpler computational models are useful for special, restricted applications. Regular expressions, for example, specify string patterns in many contexts, from office productivity software to programming languages.

Another formalism mathematically equivalent to regular expressions, Finite automata are used in circuit design and in some kinds of problem-solving. Context-free grammars specify programming language syntax. Non-deterministic pushdown automata are another formalism equivalent to context-free grammars. Primitive recursive functions are a defined subclass of the recursive functions. Different models of computation have the ability to do different tasks. One way to measure the power of a computational model is to study the class of formal languages that the model can generate; in such a way to the Chomsky hierarchy of languages is obtained.

COMPUTABILITY

Computability is the ability to solve a problem in an effective manner. It is a key topic of the field of computability theory within mathematical logic and the theory of computation within computer science. The computability of a problem is closely linked to the existence of an algorithm to solve the problem. The most widely-studied models of computability are the Turing-computable and ì-recursive functions, and the lambda calculus, all which have computationally equivalent power. Other forms of computability are studied as well: computability notions weaker than Turing machines are studied in automata theory, while computability notions stronger than Turing machines are studied in the field of hypercomputation.

Problems

A central idea in computability is that of a (computational) problem, which is a task whose computability can be explored. There are two key types of problems:

- A decision problem fixes a set *S*, which may be a set of strings, natural numbers, or other objects taken from some larger set *U*. A particular instance of the problem is to decide, given an element *u* of *U*, whether *u* is in *S*. For example, let *U* be the set of natural numbers and *S* the set of prime numbers. The corresponding decision problem corresponds to primality testing.
- A function problem consists of a function *f* from a set *U* to a set *V*. An instance of the problem is to compute, given an element *u* in *U*, the corresponding element *f*(*u*) in *V*. For example, *U* and *V* may be the set of all finite binary strings, and *f* may take a string and return the string obtained by reversing the digits of the input (so f(0101) = 1010).

Other types of problems include search problems and optimization problems. One goal of computability theory is to determine which problems, or classes of problems, can be solved in each model of computation.

Formal Models of Computation

A model of computation is a formal description of a particular type of computational process. The description often takes the form of an abstract machine that is meant to perform the task at hand. General models of computation equivalent to a Turing machine include:

Lambda Calculus

A computation consists of an initial lambda expression (or two if you want to separate the function and its input) plus a finite sequence of lambda terms, each deduced from the preceding term by one application of Beta reduction.

Combinatory Logic

Combinatory logic is a concept which has many similarities to ë-calculus, but also important differences exist (e.g. fixed point combinator Y has normal form in combinatory logic but not in ë-calculus). Combinatory logic was developed with great ambitions: understanding the nature of paradoxes, making foundations of mathematics more economic (conceptually), eliminating the notion of variables (thus clarifying their role in mathematics).

Mu-recursive Functions

A computation consists of a mu-recursive function, *i.e.* its defining sequence, any input value(s) and a sequence of recursive functions appearing in the defining sequence with inputs and outputs. Thus, if in the defining sequence of a recursive function $f(x)$ the functions $g(x)$ and $h(x,y)$ appear, then terms of the form 'g(5)=7' or 'h(3,2)=10' might appear. Each entry in this sequence needs to be an application of a basic function or follow from the entries above by using composition, primitive recursion or mu recursion. For instance if $f(x) = h(x,g(x))$, then for 'f(5)=3' to appear, terms like 'g(5)=6' and 'h(3,6)=3' must occur above. The computation terminates only if the final term gives the value of the recursive function applied to the inputs.

Markov Algorithm

a string rewriting system that uses grammar-like rules to operate on strings of symbols.

Register Machine

Register Machine is a theoretically interesting idealization of a computer. There are several variants. In most of them, each register can hold a natural number (of unlimited size), and the instructions are simple (and few in number), e.g. only decrementation (combined with conditional jump) and incrementation exist (and halting). The lack of the infinite (or dynamically growing) external store can be understood by replacing its role with Gödel numbering techniques: the fact that each register holds a natural number allows the possibility of representing a complicated thing (e.g. a sequence, or a matrix etc.) by an appropriate huge natural number — unambiguity of both representation and interpretation can be established by number theoretical foundations of these techniques.

P2 2

Like Turing machines, P2 2 uses an infinite tape of symbols (without random access), and a rather minimalistic set of instructions. But these instructions are very different, thus, unlike Turing machines, P2 2 does not need to maintain a distinct state, because all "memory-like" functionality can be provided only by the tape. Instead of rewriting the current symbol, it can perform a modular arithmetic incrementation on it. P2 2 has also a pair of instructions for a cycle, inspecting the blank symbol. Despite its minimalistic nature, it has become the parental formal language of an implemented and (for entertainment) used programming language called Brainfuck.

Turing Machine

Also similar to the finite state machine, except that the input is provided on an execution "tape", which the Turing machine can read from, write to, or move back and forth past its read/write "head". The tape is allowed to grow to arbitrary size. The Turing machine is capable of performing complex calculations which can have arbitrary duration. This model is perhaps the most important model of computation in computer science, as it simulates computation in the absence of predefined resource limits.

Multi-Tape Turing Machine

Here, there may be more than one tape; moreover there may be multiple heads per tape. Surprisingly, any computation that can be performed by this sort of machine can also be performed by an ordinary Turing machine, although the latter may be slower or require a larger total region of its tape. In addition to the general computational models, some simpler computational models are useful for special, restricted applications.

Regular expressions, for example, specify string patterns in many contexts, from office productivity software to programming languages. Another formalism mathematically equivalent to regular expressions, Finite automata are used in circuit design and in some kinds of problem-solving.

Context-free grammars specify programming language syntax. Non-deterministic pushdown automata are another formalism equivalent to context-free grammars. Different models of computation have the ability to do different tasks. One way to measure the power of a computational model is to study the class of formal languages that the model can generate; in such a way is the Chomsky hierarchy of languages is obtained. Other restricted models of computation include:

Deterministic Finite State Machine

Also called a deterministic finite automaton (DFA), or simply a finite state machine. All real computing devices in existence today can be modeled as a finite state machine, as all real computers operate on finite resources. Such a machine has a set of states, and a set of state transitions which are affected by the input stream.

Certain states are defined to be accepting states. An input stream is fed into the machine one character at a time, and the state transitions for the current state are compared to the input stream, and if there is a matching transition the machine may enter a new state. If at the end of the input stream the machine is in an accepting state, then the whole input stream is accepted.

Nondeterministic Finite State Machine

Similarly called a nondeterministic finite automaton (NFA), it is another simple model of computation, although its processing sequence is not uniquely determined. It can be interpreted as taking multiple paths of computation simultaneously through a finite number of states. However, it is possible to prove that any NFA is reducible to an equivalent DFA.

Pushdown Automaton

Similar to the finite state machine, except that it has available an execution stack, which is allowed to grow to arbitrary size. The state transitions additionally specify whether to add a symbol to the stack, or to remove a symbol from the stack.

It is more powerful than a DFA due to its infinite-memory stack, although only the top element of the stack is accessible at any time.

Power of Automata

With these computational models in hand, we can determine what their limits are. That is, what classes of languages can they accept?

Power of Finite State Machines

Computer scientists call any language that can be accepted by a finite state machine a regular language. Because of the restriction that the number of possible states in a finite state machine is finite, we can see that to find a language that is not regular, we must construct a language that would require an infinite number of states. An example of such a language is the set of all strings consisting of the letters 'a' and 'b' which contain an equal number of the letter 'a' and 'b'. To see why this language cannot be correctly recognized by a finite state machine, assume first that such a machine M exists. M must have some number of states n. Now consider the string x consisting of $(n + 1)$ 'a's followed by $(n + 1)$ 'b's. As M reads in x, there must be some state in the machine that is repeated as it reads in the first series of 'a's, since there are $(n + 1)$ 'a's and only n states by the pigeonhole principle. Call this state S, and further let d be the number of 'a's that our machine read in order to get from the first occurrence of S to some subsequent occurrence during the 'a' sequence. We know, then, that at that second occurrence of S, we can add in an additional d (where $d > 0$) 'a's and we will be again at state S. This means that we know that a string of $(n + d + 1)$ 'a's must end up in the same state as the string of $(n + 1)$ 'a's.

This implies that if our machine accepts x, it must also accept the string of $(n + d + 1)$ 'a's followed by $(n + 1)$ 'b's, which is not in the language of strings containing an equal number of 'a's and 'b's. In other words, M cannot correctly distinguish between a string of equal number of 'a's and 'b's and a string with $(n + d + 1)$ 'a's and $n + 1$ 'b's.

We know, therefore, that this language cannot be accepted correctly by any finite state machine, and is thus not a regular language. A more general form of this result is called the Pumping lemma for regular languages, which can be used to show that broad classes of languages cannot be recognized by a finite state machine.

Power of Pushdown Automata

Computer scientists define a language that can be accepted by a pushdown automaton as a Context-free language, which can be specified as a Context-free grammar. The language consisting of strings with equal numbers of 'a's and 'b's, which we showed was not a regular language, can be decided by a push-down automaton. Also, in general, a push-down automaton can behave just like a finite-state machine, so it can decide any language which is regular. This model of computation is thus strictly more powerful than finite state machines. However, it turns out there are languages that cannot be decided by push-down automaton either. The result is similar to that for regular expressions, and won't be detailed here. There exists a Pumping lemma for context-free languages. An example of such a language is the set of prime numbers.

Power of Turing Machines

Turing machines can decide any context-free language, in addition to languages not decidable by a push-down automaton, such as the language consisting of prime numbers. It is therefore a strictly more powerful model of computation. Because Turing machines have the ability to "back up" in their input tape, it is possible for a Turing machine to run for a long time in a way that is not possible with the other computation models previously described. It is possible to construct a Turing machine that will never finish running (halt) on some inputs. We say that a Turing machine can decide a language if it eventually will halt on all inputs and give an answer. A language that can be so decided is called a recursive language. We can further describe Turing machines that will eventually halt and give an answer for any input in a language, but which may run forever for input strings which are not in the language. Such Turing machines could tell us that a given string is in the language, but we may never be sure based on its behaviour that a given string is not in a language, since it may run forever in such a case. A language which is accepted by such a Turing machine is called a recursively enumerable language.

The Turing machine, it turns out, is an exceedingly powerful model of automata. Attempts to amend the definition of a Turing machine to produce a more powerful machine have surprisingly met with failure. For example, adding an extra tape to the Turing machine, giving it a 2-dimensional (or 3 or any-dimensional) infinite surface to work with can all be simulated by a Turing machine with the basic 1-dimensional tape. These models are thus not more powerful. In fact, a consequence of the Church-Turing thesis is that there is no reasonable model of computation which can decide languages that cannot be decided by a Turing machine. The question to ask then is: do there exist languages which are recursively enumerable, but not recursive? And, furthermore, are there languages which are not even recursively enumerable?

The Halting Problem

The halting problem is one of the most famous problems in computer science, because it has profound implications on the theory of computability and on how we use computers in everyday practice. The problem can be phrased: *Given a description of a Turing machine and its initial input, determine whether the programme, when executed on this input, ever halts (completes). The alternative is that it runs forever without halting.* Here we are asking not a simple question about a prime number or a palindrome, but we are instead turning the tables and asking a Turing machine to answer a question about another Turing machine. It can be shown that it is not possible to construct a Turing machine that can answer this question in all cases. That is, the only general way to know for sure if a given programme will halt on a particular input in all cases is simply to run it and see if it halts. If it does halt, then you know it halts. If it doesn't halt, however, you may never know if it will eventually halt. The language consisting of all Turing machine descriptions paired with all possible input streams on which those Turing machines will eventually halt, is not recursive. The halting problem is therefore called non-computable or undecidable. An extension of the halting problem is called Rice's Theorem, which states that it is undecidable (in general) whether a given language possesses any specific nontrivial property.

Beyond Recursively Enumerable Languages

The halting problem is easy to solve, however, if we allow that the Turing machine that decides it may run forever when given input which is a representation of a Turing machine that does not itself halt. The halting language is therefore recursively enumerable. It is possible to construct languages which are not even recursively enumerable, however. A simple example of such a language is the complement of the halting language; that is the language consisting of all Turing machines paired with input strings where the Turing machines do *not* halt on their input. To see that this language is not recursively enumerable, imagine that we construct a Turing machine *M* which is able to give a definite answer for all such Turing machines, but that it may run forever on any Turing machine that does eventually halt. We can then construct another Turing machine *M'* that simulates the operation of this machine, along with simulating directly the execution of the machine given in the input as well, by interleaving the execution of the two programmes. Since the direct simulation will eventually halt if the programme it is simulating halts, and since by assumption the simulation of *M* will eventually halt if the input programme would never halt, we know that *M'* will eventually have one of its parallel versions halt. *M'* is thus a decider for the halting problem. We have previously shown, however, that the halting problem is undecidable. We have a contradiction, and we have thus shown that our assumption that *M* exists is incorrect. The complement of the halting language is therefore not recursively enumerable.

Concurrency-Based Models

A number of computational models based on concurrency have been developed, including the Parallel Random Access Machine and the Petri net. These models of concurrent computation still do not implement any mathematical functions that cannot be implemented by Turing machines.

Stronger Models of Computation

The Church-Turing thesis conjectures that there is no effective model of computing that can compute more mathematical functions than a Turing machine. Computer scientists have imagined many varieties of hypercomputers, models of computation that go beyond Turing computability.

Oracle Machines

So-called Oracle machines have access to various "oracles" which provide the solution to specific undecidable problems. For example, the Turing machine may have a "halting oracle" which answers immediately whether a given Turing machine will ever halt on a given input. These machines are a central topic of study in recursion theory.

Limits of Hyper-Computation

Even these machines, which seemingly represent the

limit of automata that we could imagine, run into their own limitations. While each of them can solve the halting problem for a Turing machine, they cannot solve their own version of the halting problem. For example, an Oracle machine cannot answer the question of whether a given Oracle machine will ever halt.

COMPUTATIONAL COMPLEXITY THEORY

Computational complexity theory is a branch of the theory of computation in theoretical computer science and mathematics that focuses on classifying computational problems according to their inherent difficulty. In this context, a computational problem is understood to be a task that is in principle amenable to being solved by a computer (which basically means that the problem can be stated by a set of mathematical instructions). Informally, a computational problem consists of problem instances and solutions to these problem instances. For example, primality testing is the problem of determining whether a given number is prime or not. The instances of this problem are natural numbers, and the solution to an instance is *yes* or *no* based on whether the number is prime or not. A problem is regarded as inherently difficult if solving the problem requires a large amount of resources, whatever the algorithm used for solving it. The theory formalizes this intuition, by introducing mathematical models of computation to study these problems and quantifying the amount of resources needed to solve them, such as time and storage. Other complexity measures are also used, such as the amount of communication (used in communication complexity), the number of gates in a circuit (used in circuit complexity) and the number of processors (used in parallel computing). One of the roles of computational complexity theory is to determine the practical limits on what computers can and cannot do.

Closely related fields in theoretical computer science

are analysis of algorithms and computability theory. A key distinction between analysis of algorithms and computational complexity theory is that the former is devoted to analyzing the amount of resources needed by a particular algorithm to solve a problem, whereas the latter asks a more general question about all possible algorithms that could be used to solve the same problem. More precisely, it tries to classify problems that can or cannot be solved with appropriately restricted resources. In turn, imposing restrictions on the available resources is what distinguishes computational complexity from computability theory: the latter theory asks what kind of problems can be solved in principle algorithmically.

Computational Problems

Problem Instances

A computational problem can be viewed as an infinite collection of *instances* together with a *solution* for every instance. The input string for a computational problem is referred to as a problem instance, and should not be confused with the problem itself. In computational complexity theory, a problem refers to the abstract question to be solved. In contrast, an instance of this problem is a rather concrete utterance, which can serve as the input for a decision problem. For example, consider the problem of primality testing. The instance is a number and the solution is "yes" if the number is prime and "no" otherwise. Alternately, the instance is a particular input to the problem, and the solution is the output corresponding to the given input. To further highlight the difference between a problem and an instance, consider the following instance of the decision version of the traveling salesman problem: Is there a route of length at most 2000 kilometres passing through all of Germany's 15 largest cities? The answer to this particular problem instance is of little use for solving other instances of the problem, such as asking for a round trip through all sites in Milan whose total length is at most 10 km. For this reason, complexity theory addresses computational problems and not particular problem instances.

Representing Problem Instances

When considering computational problems, a problem instance is a string over an alphabet. Usually, the alphabet is taken to be the binary alphabet (i.e., the set {0,1}), and thus the strings are bitstrings. As in a real-world computer, mathematical objects other than bitstrings must be suitably encoded. For example, integers can be represented in binary notation, and graphs can be encoded directly via their adjacency matrices, or by encoding their adjacency lists in binary. Even though some proofs of complexity-theoretic theorems regularly assume some concrete choice of input encoding, one tries to keep the discussion abstract enough to be independent of the choice of encoding. This can be achieved by ensuring that different representations can be transformed into each other efficiently.

Decision Problems as Formal Languages

Decision problems are one of the central objects of study in computational complexity theory. A decision problem is a special type of computational problem whose answer is either *yes* or *no*, or alternately either 1 or 0. A decision problem can be viewed as a formal language, where the members of the language are instances whose answer is yes, and the non-members are those instances whose output is no. The objective is to decide, with the aid of an algorithm, whether a given input string is member of the formal language under consideration. If the algorithm deciding this problem returns the answer *yes*, the algorithm is said to accept the input string, otherwise it is said to reject the input. An example of a decision problem is the following. The input is an arbitrary graph. The problem consists in deciding whether the given graph is connected, or not. The formal language associated with this decision problem is then the set of all connected graphs—of course, to obtain a precise definition of this language, one has to decide how graphs are encoded as binary strings.

Function Problems

A function problem is a computational problem where a single output (of a total function) is expected for every input, but the output is more complex than that of a decision problem, that is, it isn't just yes or no. Notable examples include the traveling salesman problem and the integer factorization problem. It is tempting to think that the notion of function problems is much richer than the notion of decision problems. However, this is not really the case, since function problems can be recast as decision problems. For example, the multiplication of two integers can be expressed as the set of triples (a, b, c) such that the relation $a \times b = c$ holds. Deciding whether a given triple is member of this set corresponds to solving the problem of multiplying two numbers.

Measuring the Size of an Instance

To measure the difficulty of solving a computational problem, one may wish to see how much time the best algorithm requires to solve the problem. However, the running time may, in general, depend on the instance. In particular, larger instances will require more time to solve. Thus the time required to solve a problem (or the space required, or any measure of complexity) is calculated as function of the size of the instance. This is usually taken to be the size of the input in bits. Complexity theory is interested in how algorithms scale with an increase in the input size. For instance, in the problem of finding whether a graph is connected, how much more time does it take to solve a problem for a graph with $2n$ vertices compared to the time taken for a graph with n vertices? If the input size is n, the time taken can be expressed as a function of n. Since the time taken on different inputs of the same size can be different, the worst-case time complexity T(n) is defined to be the maximum time taken over all inputs of size n. If T(n) is a polynomial in n, then the algorithm is said to be a polynomial time algorithm. Cobham's thesis says that a problem can be solved with a feasible amount of resources if it admits a polynomial time algorithm.

Machine Models and Complexity Measures

Turing Machine

A Turing machine is a mathematical model of a general computing machine. It is a theoretical device that manipulates symbols contained on a strip of tape. Turing machines are not intended as a practical computing technology, but rather as a thought experiment representing a computing machine. It is believed that if a problem can be solved by an algorithm, there exists a Turing machine that solves the problem. Indeed, this is the statement of the Church–Turing thesis. Furthermore, it is known that everything that can be computed on other models of computation known to us today, such as a RAM machine, Conway's Game of Life, cellular automata or any programming language can be computed on a Turing machine. Since Turing machines are easy to analyze mathematically, and are believed to be as powerful as any other model of computation, the Turing machine is the most commonly used model in complexity theory. Many types of Turing machines are used to define complexity classes, such as deterministic Turing machines, probabilistic Turing machines, non-deterministic Turing machines, quantum Turing machines, symmetric Turing machines and alternating Turing machines. They are all equally powerful in principle, but when resources (such as time or space) are bounded, some of these may be more powerful than others.

A deterministic Turing machine is the most basic Turing machine, which uses a fixed set of rules to determine its future actions. A probabilistic Turing machine is a deterministic Turing machine with an extra supply of random bits. The ability to make probabilistic decisions often helps algorithms solve problems more efficiently. Algorithms that use random bits are called randomized algorithms. A non-deterministic Turing machine is a deterministic Turing machine with an added feature of non-determinism, which allows a Turing machine to have multiple possible future actions from a given state. One way to view non-determinism is that the Turing machine branches into many possible computational paths at each step, and if it solves the problem in any of these branches, it is said to have solved the problem. Clearly, this model is not meant to be a physically realizable model, it is just a theoretically interesting abstract machine that gives rise to particularly interesting complexity classes. For examples, see nondeterministic algorithm.

Other Machine Models

Many machine models different from the standard multi-tape Turing machines have been proposed in the literature, for example random access machines. Perhaps surprisingly, each of these models can be converted to another without providing any extra computational power. The time and memory consumption of these alternate models may vary. What all these models have in common is that the machines operate deterministically. However, some computational problems are easier to analyze in terms of more unusual resources. For example, a nondeterministic Turing machine is a computational model that is allowed to branch out to check many different possibilities at once. The nondeterministic Turing machine has very little to do with how we physically want to compute algorithms, but its branching exactly captures many of the mathematical models we want to analyze, so that nondeterministic time is a very important resource in analyzing computational problems.

Complexity Measures

For a precise definition of what it means to solve a problem using a given amount of time and space, a computational model such as the deterministic Turing machine is used. The *time required* by a deterministic Turing machine M on input x is the total number of state transitions, or steps, the machine makes before it halts and outputs the answer ("yes" or "no"). A Turing machine M is said to operate within time $f(n)$, if the time required by M on each input of length n is at most $f(n)$. A decision problem A can be solved in time $f(n)$ if there exists a Turing machine operating in time $f(n)$ that solves the problem. Since complexity theory is interested in classifying problems based on their difficulty, one defines sets of problems based on some criteria. For instance, the set of problems solvable within time $f(n)$ on a deterministic Turing machine is then denoted by DTIME($f(n)$). Analogous definitions can be made for space requirements. Although time and space are the most well-known complexity resources, any complexity measure can be viewed as a computational resource. Complexity measures are very generally defined by the Blum complexity axioms. Other complexity measures used in complexity theory include communication complexity, circuit complexity, and decision tree complexity.

Best, Worst and Average Case Complexity

The best, worst and average case complexity refer to three different ways of measuring the time complexity (or any other complexity measure) of different inputs of the same size. Since some inputs of size n may be faster to solve than others, we define the following complexities:

- Best-case complexity: This is the complexity of solving the problem for the best input of size n.
- Worst-case complexity: This is the complexity of solving the problem for the worst input of size n.

- Average-case complexity: This is the complexity of solving the problem on an average. This complexity is only defined with respect to a probability distribution over the inputs. For instance, if all inputs of the same size are assumed to be equally likely to appear, the average case complexity can be defined with respect to the uniform distribution over all inputs of size n.

For example, consider the deterministic sorting algorithm quicksort. This solves the problem of sorting a list of integers that is given as the input. The best-case scenario is when the input is already sorted, and the algorithm takes time $O(n \log n)$ for such inputs. The worst-case is when the input is sorted in reverse order, and the algorithm takes time $O(n^2)$ for this case. If we assume that all possible permutations of the input list are equally likely, the average time taken for sorting is $O(n \log n)$.

Upper and Lower Bounds on the Complexity of Problems

To classify the computation time (or similar resources, such as space consumption), one is interested in proving upper and lower bounds on the minimum amount of time required by the most efficient algorithm solving a given problem. The complexity of an algorithm is usually taken to be its worst-case complexity, unless specified otherwise. Analyzing a particular algorithm falls under the field of analysis of algorithms. To show an upper bound $T(n)$ on the time complexity of a problem, one needs to show only that there is a particular algorithm with running time at most $T(n)$. However, proving lower bounds is much more difficult, since lower bounds make a statement about all possible algorithms that solve a given problem. The phrase "all possible algorithms" includes not just the algorithms known today, but any algorithm that might be discovered in the future. To show a lower bound of $T(n)$ for a problem requires showing that no algorithm can have time complexity lower than $T(n)$. Upper and lower bounds are usually stated using the big Oh notation, which hides constant factors and smaller terms. This makes the bounds independent of the specific details of the computational model used. For instance, if $T(n) = 7n^2 + 15n + 40$, in big Oh notation one would write $T(n) = O(n^2)$.

Complexity Classes

Defining Complexity Classes

A complexity class is a set of problems of related complexity. Simpler complexity classes are defined by the following factors:

- The type of computational problem: The most commonly used problems are decision problems. However, complexity classes can be defined based on function problems, counting problems, optimization problems, promise problems, etc.
- The model of computation: The most common model of computation is the deterministic Turing machine, but many complexity classes are based on nondeterministic Turing machines, Boolean circuits, quantum Turing machines, monotone circuits, etc.
- The resource (or resources) that are being bounded and the bounds: These two properties are usually stated together, such as "polynomial time", "logarithmic space", "constant depth", etc.

Of course, some complexity classes have complex definitions that do not fit into this framework. Thus, a typical complexity class has a definition like the following: The set of decision problems solvable by a deterministic Turing machine within time $f(n)$. (This complexity class is known as DTIME($f(n)$).) But bounding the computation time above by some concrete function $f(n)$ often yields complexity classes that depend on the chosen machine model. For instance, the language $\{xx \mid x \text{ is any binary string}\}$ can be solved in linear time on a multi-tape Turing machine, but necessarily requires quadratic time in the model of single-tape Turing machines. If we allow polynomial variations in running time, Cobham-Edmonds thesis states that "the time complexities in any two reasonable and general models of computation are polynomially related" (Goldreich 2008, Chapter 1.2). This forms the basis for the complexity class P, which is the set of decision problems solvable by a deterministic Turing machine within polynomial time. The corresponding set of function problems is FP.

Important Complexity Classes

Many important complexity classes can be defined by bounding the time or space used by the algorithm. Some important complexity classes of decision problems. Other important complexity classes include BPP, ZPP and RP, which are defined using probabilistic Turing machines; AC and NC, which are defined using Boolean circuits and BQP and QMA, which are defined using quantum Turing machines. #P is an important complexity class of counting problems (not decision problems). Classes like IP and AM are defined using Interactive proof systems. ALL is the class of all decision problems.

Reduction

Many complexity classes are defined using the concept of a reduction. A reduction is a transformation of one problem into another problem. It captures the informal notion of a problem being at least as difficult as another problem. For instance, if a problem X can be solved using an algorithm for Y, X is no more difficult than Y, and we say that X *reduces* to Y. There are many different types of reductions, based on the method of reduction, such as Cook reductions, Karp reductions and Levin reductions, and the bound on the complexity of reductions, such as polynomial-time reductions or log-space reductions. The most commonly used reduction is a polynomial-time reduction. This means that the reduction process takes polynomial time. For example, the problem of squaring an integer can be reduced to the problem of multiplying two integers. This means an algorithm for multiplying two integers can be used to square an integer. Indeed, this can be done by giving the same input to both inputs of the multiplication algorithm. Thus we see that squaring is not more difficult than multiplication, since squaring can be reduced to multiplication.

This motivates the concept of a problem being hard for a complexity class. A problem X is *hard* for a class of problems C if every problem in C can be reduced to X. Thus no problem in C is harder than X, since an algorithm for X allows us to solve any problem in C. Of course, the notion of hard problems depends on the type of reduction being used. For complexity classes larger than P, polynomial-time reductions are commonly used. In particular, the set of problems that are hard for NP is the set of NP-hard problems.

If a problem X is in C and hard for C, then X is said to be *complete* for C. This means that X is the hardest problem in C. (Since many problems could be equally hard, one might say that X is one of the hardest problems in C.) Thus the class of NP-complete problems contains the most difficult problems in NP, in the sense that they are the ones most likely not to be in P. Because the problem P = NP is not solved, being able to reduce a known NP-complete problem, $Đ_2$, to another problem, $Đ_1$, would indicate that there is no known polynomial-time solution for $Đ_1$.

This is because a polynomial-time solution to $Đ_1$ would yield a polynomial-time solution to $Đ_2$. Similarly, because all NP problems can be reduced to the set, finding an NP-complete problem that can be solved in polynomial time would mean that P = NP.

Important Open Problems

P Versus NP Problem

The complexity class P is often seen as a mathematical abstraction modeling those computational tasks that admit an efficient algorithm. This hypothesis is called the Cobham–Edmonds thesis. The complexity class NP, on the other hand, contains many problems that people would like to solve efficiently, but for which no efficient algorithm is known, such as the Boolean satisfiability problem, the Hamiltonian path problem and the vertex cover problem. Since deterministic Turing machines are special nondeterministic Turing machines, it is easily observed that each problem in P is also member of the class NP. The question of whether P equals NP is one of the most important open questions in theoretical computer science because of the wide implications of a solution. If the answer is yes, many important problems can be shown to have more efficient solutions. These include various types of integer programming problems in operations research, many problems in logistics, protein structure prediction in biology, and the ability to find formal proofs of pure mathematics theorems. The P versus NP problem is one of the Millennium Prize Problems proposed by the Clay Mathematics Institute. There is a US$1,000,000 prize for resolving the problem.

Problems in NP Not Known to be in P or NP-Complete

It was shown by Ladner that if P "" NP then there exist problems in NP that are neither in P nor NP-complete. Such problems are called NP-intermediate problems. The graph isomorphism problem, the discrete logarithm problem and the integer factorization problem are examples of problems believed to be NP-intermediate. They are some of the very few NP problems not known to be in P or to be NP-complete. The graph isomorphism problem is the computational problem of determining whether two finite graphs are isomorphic. An important unsolved problem in complexity theory is whether the graph isomorphism problem is in P, NP-complete, or NP-intermediate. The answer is not known, but it is believed that the problem is at least not NP-complete. If graph isomorphism is NP-complete, the polynomial time hierarchy collapses to its second level. Since it is widely believed that the polynomial hierarchy does not collapse to any finite level, it is believed that graph isomorphism is not NP-complete.

The best algorithm for this problem, due to Laszlo Babai and Eugene Luks has run time $2^{O(“(n \log n))}$ for graphs with n vertices. The integer factorization problem is the computational problem of determining the prime factorization of a given integer. Phrased as a decision problem, it is the problem of deciding whether the input has a factor less than k. No efficient integer factorization algorithm is known, and this fact forms the basis of several modern cryptographic systems, such as the RSA algorithm. The integer factorization problem is in NP and in co-NP (and even in UP and co-UP). If the problem is NP-complete, the polynomial time hierarchy will collapse to its first level (i.e., NP will equal co-NP). The best known algorithm for integer factorization is the general number field sieve, which takes time $O(e^{(64/9)1/3(n.\log 2)1/3(\log (n.\log 2))2/3})$ to factor an n-bit integer. However, the best known quantum algorithm for this problem, Shor's algorithm, does run in polynomial time. Unfortunately, this fact doesn't say much about where the problem lies with respect to non-quantum complexity classes.

Separations Between Other Complexity Classes

Many known complexity classes are suspected to be unequal, but this has not been proved. For instance P” NP” PP” PSPACE, but it is possible that P = PSPACE. If P is not equal to NP, then P is not equal to PSPACE either. Since there are many known complexity classes between P and PSPACE, such as RP, BPP, PP, BQP, MA, PH, etc., it is possible that all these complexity classes collapse to one class. Proving that any of these classes are unequal would be a major breakthrough in complexity theory. Along the same lines, co-NP is the class containing the complement problems (i.e. problems with the *yes/no* answers reversed) of NP problems. It is believed that NP is not equal to co-NP; however, it has not yet been proven. It has been shown that if these two complexity classes are not equal then P is not equal to NP. Similarly, it is not known if L (the set of all problems that can be solved in logarithmic space) is strictly contained in P or equal to P. Again, there are many complexity classes between the two, such as NL and NC, and it is not known if they are distinct or equal classes.

Intractability

Problems that can be solved but not fast enough for the solution to be useful are called *intractable*. In complexity theory, problems that lack polynomial-time solutions are considered to be intractable for more than the smallest inputs. In fact, the Cobham–Edmonds thesis states that only those problems that can be solved in polynomial time can be feasibly computed on some computational device. Problems that are known to be intractable in this sense include those that are EXPTIME-hard. If NP is not the same as P, then the NP-complete problems are also intractable in this sense. To see why exponential-time algorithms might be unusable in practice, consider a programme that makes 2^n operations before halting. For small n, say 100, and assuming for the sake of example that the computer does 10^{12} operations each second, the programme would run for about 4×10^{10} years, which is roughly the age of the universe. Even with a much faster computer, the programme would only be useful for very small instances and in that sense the intractability of a problem is somewhat independent of technological progress. Nevertheless a polynomial time algorithm is not always practical.

If its running time is, say, n^{15}, it is unreasonable to consider it efficient and it is still useless except on small instances. What intractability means in practice is open to debate. Saying that a problem is not in P does not imply that all large cases of the problem are hard or even that most of them are. For example the decision problem in Presburger arithmetic has been shown not to be in P, yet algorithms have been written that solve the problem in reasonable times in most cases. Similarly, algorithms can solve the NP-complete knapsack problem over a wide range of sizes in less than quadratic time and SAT solvers routinely handle large instances of the NP-complete Boolean satisfiability problem.

Continuous Complexity Theory

Continuous complexity theory can refer to complexity theory of problems that involve continuous functions that are approximated by discretizations, as studied in numerical analysis. One approach to complexity theory of numerical analysis is information based complexity. Continuous complexity theory can also refer to complexity theory of the use of analog computation, which uses continuous dynamical systems and differential equations. Control theory can be considered a form of computation and differential equations are used in the modelling of continuous-time and hybrid discrete-continuous-time systems.

History

Before the actual research explicitly devoted to the complexity of algorithmic problems started off, numerous foundations were laid out by various researchers. Most influential among these was the definition of Turing machines by Alan Turing in 1936, which turned out to be a very robust and flexible notion of computer. Fortnow & Homer (2003) date the beginning of systematic studies in computational complexity to the seminal paper "On the Computational Complexity of Algorithms" by Juris

Hartmanis and Richard Stearns (1965), which laid out the definitions of time and space complexity and proved the hierarchy theorems. According to Fortnow & Homer (2003), earlier papers studying problems solvable by Turing machines with specific bounded resources include John Myhill's definition of linear bounded automata (Myhill 1960), Raymond Smullyan's study of rudimentary sets (1961), as well as Hisao Yamada's paper on real-time computations (1962). Somewhat earlier, Boris Trakhtenbrot (1956), a pioneer in the field from the USSR, studied another specific complexity measure. As he remembers:

> However, [my] initial interest [in automata theory] was increasingly set aside in favour of computational complexity, an exciting fusion of combinatorial methods, inherited from switching theory, with the conceptual arsenal of the theory of algorithms. These ideas had occurred to me earlier in 1955 when I coined the term "signalizing function", which is nowadays commonly known as "complexity measure".
>
> —Boris Trakhtenbrot, From Logic to Theoretical Computer Science – An Update. In: *Pillars of Computer Science*, LNCS 4800, Springer 2008.

In 1967, Manuel Blum developed an axiomatic complexity theory based on his axioms and proved an important result, the so called, speed-up theorem. The field really began to flourish when the US researcher Stephen Cook and, working independently, Leonid Levin in the USSR, proved that there exist practically relevant problems that are NP-complete.

In 1972, Richard Karp took this idea a leap forward with his landmark paper, "Reducibility Among Combinatorial Problems", in which he showed that 21 diverse combinatorial and graph theoretical problems, each infamous for its computational intractability, are NP-complete.

MODEL OF COMPUTATION

In computability theory and computational complexity theory, a model of computation is the definition of the set of allowable operations used in computation and their respective costs. It is used for measuring the complexity of an algorithm in execution time and or memory space: by assuming a certain model of computation, it is possible to analyze the computational resources required or to discuss the limitations of algorithms or computers.

Some examples of models include Turing machines, recursive functions, lambda calculus, and production systems. In model-driven engineering, the model of computation explains how the behaviour of the whole system is the result of the behaviour of each of its components. In the field of runtime analysis of algorithms, it is common to specify a computational model in terms of *primitive operations* allowed which have unit cost, or simply unit-cost operations.

A commonly used example is the random access machine, which has unit cost for read and write access to all of its memory cells. In this respect, it differs from the above mentioned Turing machine model.

There are many models of computation, differing in the set of admissible operations and their computations cost. They fall into the following broad categories: abstract machine, used in proofs of computability and upper bounds on computational complexity of algorithms, and decision tree models, used in proofs of lower bounds on computational complexity of algorithmic problems. A key point which is often overlooked is that published lower bounds for problems are often given for a model of computation that is more restricted than the set of operations that you could use in practice and therefore there are algorithms that are faster than what would naively be thought possible.

PARTIAL FUNCTION

In mathematics, a partial function from X to Y is a function f: X' '! Y, where X' is a subset of X. It generalizes the concept of a function by not forcing f to map *every* element of X to an element of Y (only some subset X' of X). If $X' = X$, then f is called a total function and is equivalent to a function. Partial functions are often used when the exact domain, X', is not known (e.g. many functions in computability theory). Specifically, we will say that for any x " X, either:

- $f(x) = y$ " Y (it is defined as a single element in Y) or
- $f(x)$ is undefined.

Domain of a Partial Function

There are two distinct meanings in current mathematical usage for the notion of the domain of a partial function. Most mathematicians, including recursion theorists, use the term "domain of f" for the set of all values x such that $f(x)$ is defined (X' above). But some, particularly category theorists, consider the domain of a partial function f:X'!Y to be X, and refer to X' as the domain of definition. Occasionally, a partial function with domain X and codomain Y is written as f: X ø! Y, using an arrow with vertical stroke. A partial function is said to be injective or surjective when the total function given by the restriction of the partial function to its domain of definition is. A partial function may be both injective and surjective, but the term bijection generally only applies to total functions. An injective partial function may be inverted to an injective partial function, and a partial function which is both injective and surjective has an injective function as inverse.

Discussion and Examples

A partial function that is not a total function since the

element 1 in the left-hand set is not associated with anything in the right-hand set.

Natural Logarithm

Consider the natural logarithm function mapping the real numbers to themselves. The logarithm of a non-positive real is not a real number, so the natural logarithm function doesn't associate any real number in the codomain with any non-positive real number in the domain. Therefore, the natural logarithm function is not a total function when viewed as a function from the reals to themselves, but it is a partial function. If the domain is restricted to only include the positive reals (that is, if the natural logarithm function is viewed as a function from the positive reals to the reals), then the natural logarithm is a total function.

Bottom Type

In some automated theorem proving systems a partial function is considered as returning the bottom type when it is undefined. The Curry-Howard correspondence uses this to map proofs and computer programmes to each other. In computer science a partial function corresponds to a subroutine that raises an exception or loops forever. The IEEE floating point standard defines a Not-a-number value which is returned when a floating point operation is undefined and exceptions are suppressed, e.g. when the square root of a negative number is requested.

REFERENCES

Arvind, Vikraman; Kurur, Piyush P. (2006), "Graph isomorphism is in SPP", *Information and Computation* 204 (5): 835–852,

Berger, Bonnie A.; Leighton, T (1998), "Protein folding in the hydrophobic-hydrophilic (HP) model is NP-complete", *Journal of Computational Biology* 5 (1): p27–40,

Boaz Barak's course on Computational Complexity Lecture 2

Christos Papadimitriou (1993). *Computational Complexity* (1st ed.). Addison Wesley. ISBN 0-201-53082-1. Chapter 3: Computability, pp. 57–70.

Complexity Theory and Numerical Analysis, Steve Smale, Acta Numerica, 1997 - Cambridge Univ Press

Computational Techniques for the Verification of Hybrid Systems, Claire J. Tomlin, Ian Mitchell, Alexandre M. Bayen, Meeko Oishi, Proceedings of the IEEE, Vol. 91, No. 7, July 2003.

Cook, Stephen (April 2000), *The P versus NP Problem*, Clay Mathematics Institute,

Eitan Gurari (1989). *An Introduction to the Theory of Computation*. Computer Science Press.

Hein, James L. (1996) *Theory of Computation*. Sudbury, MA: Jones & Bartlett.

Hopcroft, J.E., Motwani, R. and Ullman, J.D. (2007) Introduction to Automata Theory, Languages, and Computation, Addison Wesley, Boston/San Francisco/New York (page 368)

Hopcroft, John E., and Jeffrey D. Ullman (2006). *Introduction to Automata Theory, Languages, and Computation. 3rd ed* Reading, MA: Addison-Wesley.

Jaffe, Arthur M. (2006), "The Millennium Grand Challenge in Mathematics", *Notices of the AMS* 53 (6),

Ladner, Richard E. (1975), "On the structure of polynomial time reducibility" (PDF), *Journal of the ACM (JACM)* 22 (1): 151–171,

Lance Fortnow. Computational Complexity Blog: Complexity Class of the Week: Factoring. September 13, 2002.

Lewis, F. D. (2007). *Essentials of theoretical computer science* A textbook covering the topics of formal languages, automata and grammars. The emphasis appears to be on presenting an overview of the results and their applications rather than providing proofs of the results.

Martin Davis, Ron Sigal, Elaine J. Weyuker, *Computability, complexity, and languages: fundamentals of theoretical computer science*, 2nd ed., Academic Press, 1994.

Michael Sipser (1997). *Introduction to the Theory of Computation*. PWS Publishing. ISBN 0-534-94728-X. Part Two: Computability Theory, Chapters 3–6, pp. 123–222.

Michael Sipser (2006). *Introduction to the Theory of Computation 2ed*. PWS Publishing.

Richard M. Karp (1972), "Reducibility Among Combinatorial Problems", in R. E. Miller and J. W. Thatcher (editors), *Complexity of Computer Computations*, New York: Plenum, pp. 85–103.

S. Barry Cooper (2004). *Computability Theory* (1st ed.). Chapman & Hall/CRC. ISBN 978-1584882374.

Taylor, R. Gregory (1998). *Models of Computation and Formal Languages*. New York: Oxford University Press.

Trakhtenbrot, B.A.: Signalizing functions and tabular operators. Uchionnye Zapiski Penzenskogo Pedinstituta (Transactions of the Penza Pedagogoical Institute) 4, 75–87 (1956) (in Russian)

Uwe Schöning, "Graph isomorphism is in the low hierarchy", Proceedings of the 4th Annual Symposium on Theoretical Aspects of Computer Science, 1987, 114–124; also: *Journal of Computer and System Sciences*, vol. 37 (1988), 312–323

Yamada, H. (1962). "Real-Time Computation and Recursive Functions Not Real-Time Computable". *IEEE Transactions on Electronic Computers* EC-11: 753.

6

Focus on Empirical Algorithm and Medical Algorithm

EMPIRICAL ALGORITHMICS

Empirical algorithmics (sometimes also called *experimental algorithmics*) is the area within computer science that uses empirical methods to study the behaviour of algorithms. It can be used in the analysis of algorithms. Methods from empirical algorithmics complement theoretical methods for the analysis of algorithms. Through the principled application of empirical methods, particularly from statistics, it is often possible to obtain insights into the behaviour of algorithms that are (currently) inaccessible to theoretical analysis, in particular, high-performance heuristic algorithms for hard combinatorial problems.

Empirical methods can also be used to achieve substantial improvements in algorithmic efficiency. There are two main branches of empirical algorithmics: the first (known as *empirical analysis*) deals with the analysis and characterisation of the behaviour of algorithms, and the second (known as *algorithm design* or *algorithm engineering*) is focused on empirical methods for improving the performance of algorithms. The former uses mostly techniques and tools from statistics, while the latter is based on approaches from statistics, machine learning and optimization.

Research in empirical algorithmics is published in several journals, including the ACM Journal on Experimental Algorithmics (JEA) and the Journal of Artificial Intelligence Research (JAIR), as well as at numerous conferences, including SEA, WEA, AAAI, IJCAI, CP and SLS. Well-known researchers in empirical algorithmics include Marco Chiarandini, Catherine McGeoch, Carla Gomes, Holger H. Hoos, David S. Johnson, Kevin Leyton-Brown, Ruben Ruiz, Bart Selman, Thomas Stützle and Roberto Battiti.

MEDICAL ALGORITHM

A medical algorithm is any computation, formula, statistical survey, nomogram, or look-up table, useful in healthcare. Medical algorithms include decision tree approaches to healthcare treatment (i.e., if symptoms A, B, and C are evident, then use treatment X) and also less clear-cut tools aimed at reducing or defining uncertainty.

Scope

Medical algorithms are part of a broader field which is usually fit under the aims of medical informatics and medical decision making. Medical decisions occur in several areas of medical activity including medical test selection, diagnosis, therapy and prognosis, and automatic control of medical equipment. In relation to logic-based and artificial neural network-based clinical decision support system, which are also computer applications to the medical decision making field, algorithms are less complex in architecture, data structure and user interface. Medical algorithms are not necessarily implemented using digital computers. In fact, many of them can be represented on paper, in the form of diagrams, nomographs, etc.

Examples

A wealth of medical information exists in the form of published medical algorithms. These algorithms range from simple calculations to complex outcome predictions. Most clinicians use only a small subset routinely.

Examples of medical algorithms are:

- Calculators,. e.g., an on-line or stand-alone calculator for body mass index (BMI) when stature and body weight are given;
- Flowcharts, e.g., a binary decision tree for deciding what is the etiology of chest pain
- Look-up tables, e.g., for looking up food energy and nutritional contents of foodstuffs
- Nomographs, e.g., a moving circular slide to calculate body surface area or drug dosages.

A common class of algorithms are embedded in guidelines on the choice of treatments produced by many national, state, financial and local healthcare organizations and provided as knowledge resources for day to day use and for induction of new physicians. A field which has gained particular attention is the choice of medications for psychiatric conditions. In the United Kingdom guidelines or algorithms for this have been produced by most of the circa 500 primary care trusts, substantially all of the circa 100 secondary care psychiatric units and many of the circa 10 000 general practices. In the US there is a national (federal) initiative to provide them for all states, and by 2005 six states were adapting the approach of the Texas Medication Algorithm Project or otherwise working on their production. A grammar — the Arden syntax — exists for describing algorithms in terms of medical logic modules. An approach such as this should allow exchange of MLMs between doctors and establishments, and enrichment of the common stock of tools.

Purpose

The intended purpose of medical algorithms is to improve and standardize decisions made in the delivery of medical care. Medical algorithms assist in standardizing selection and application of treatment regimens, with algorithm automation intended to reduce potential introduction of errors. Some attempt to predict the outcome, for example critical care scoring systems. Computerized algorithms can provide timely clinical decision support, improve adherence to evidence-based guidelines, and be a resource for education and research. Medical algorithms based on best practice can assist everyone involved in delivery of standardized treatment via a wide range of clinical care providers. Many are presented as protocols and it is a key task in training to ensure people step outside the protocol when necessary. In our present state of knowledge, generating hints and producing guidelines may be less satisfying to the authors, but more appropriate.

Cautions

In common with most science and medicine, algorithms whose contents are not wholly available for scrutiny and open to improvement should be regarded with suspicion. Computations obtained from medical algorithms should be compared with, and tempered by, clinical knowledge and physician judgment.

7

Data Structure and Concurrent Data Structure: An Introductory Overview

DATA STRUCTURE

In computer science, a data structure is a particular way of storing and organizing data in a computer so that it can be used efficiently. Different kinds of data structures are suited to different kinds of applications, and some are highly specialized to specific tasks. For example, B-trees are particularly well-suited for implementation of databases, while compiler implementations usually use hash tables to look up identifiers. Data structures are used in almost every programme or software system. Data structures provide a means to manage huge amounts of data efficiently, such as large databases and internet indexing services. Usually, efficient data structures are a key to designing efficient algorithms. Some formal design methods and programming languages emphasize data structures, rather than algorithms, as the key organizing factor in software design.

Basic Principles

Data structures are generally based on the ability of a computer to fetch and store data at any place in its memory, specified by an address — a bit string that can be itself stored in memory and manipulated by the programme. Thus the record and array data structures are based on computing the addresses of data items with arithmetic operations; while the linked data structures are based on storing addresses of data items within the structure itself. Many data structures use both principles, sometimes combined in non-trivial ways (as in XOR linking) The implementation of a data structure usually requires writing a set of procedures that create and manipulate instances of that structure. The efficiency of a data structure cannot be analyzed separately from those operations. This observation motivates the theoretical concept of an abstract data type, a data structure that is defined indirectly by the operations that may be performed on it, and the mathematical properties of those operations (including their space and time cost).

Common Data Structures

Common data structures include: array, linked list, hash-table, heap, B-tree, red-black tree, trie.

Language Support

Most Assembly languages and some low-level languages, such as BCPL, generally lack support for data structures. Many high-level programming languages, and some higher-level assembly languages, such as MASM, on the other hand, have special syntax or other built-in support for certain data structures, such as vectors (one-dimensional arrays) in the C language and multi-dimensional arrays in Pascal. Most programming languages feature some sort of library mechanism that allows data structure implementations to be reused by different programmes. Modern languages usually come with standard libraries that implement the most common data structures. Examples are the C++ Standard Template Library, the Java Collections Framework, and Microsoft's .NET Framework. Modern languages also generally support modular programming, the separation between the interface of a library module and its implementation. Some provide opaque data types that allow clients to hide implementation details. Object-oriented programming languages, such as C++, Java and .NET Framework use classes for this purpose. Many known data structures have concurrent versions that allow multiple computing threads to access the data structure simultaneously.

CONCURRENT DATA STRUCTURE

In computer science, a concurrent data structure is a particular way of storing and organizing data for access by multiple computing threads (or processes) on a computer. Historically, such data structures were used on uniprocessor machines with operating systems that supported multiple computing threads (or processes). The term concurrency captured the multiplexing/interleaving of the threads' operations on the data by the operating system, even though the processors never issued two operations that accessed the data simultaneously. Today, as multiprocessor computer architectures that provide parallelism become the dominant computing platform (through the proliferation of multi-core processors), the term has come to stand mainly for data structures that can be accessed by multiple threads which may actually access the data simultaneously because they run on different processors that communicate with one another. The concurrent data structure (sometimes also called a shared data structure) is usually considered to reside in an abstract storage environment called shared memory, though this memory may be physically implemented as either a "tightly coupled" or a distributed collection of storage modules.

Basic Principles

Concurrent data structures, intended for use in parallel or distributed computing environments, differ from "sequential" data structures, intended for use on a uniprocessor machine, in several ways. Most notably, in a sequential environment one specifies the data structure's properties and checks that they are implemented correctly, by providing safety properties. In a concurrent environment, the specification must also describe liveness properties which an implementation must provide. Safety properties usually state that something bad never happens, while liveness properties state that something good keeps happening. These properties can be expressed, for example, using Linear Temporal Logic. The type of liveness requirements tend to define the data structure. The method calls can be blocking or non-blocking. Data structures are not restricted to one type or the other, and can allow combinations where some method calls are blocking and others are non-blocking (examples can be found in the Java concurrency software library).

The safety properties of concurrent data structures must capture their behaviour given the many possible interleavings of methods called by different threads. It is quite intuitive to specify how abstract data structures behave in a sequential setting in which there are no interleavings. Therefore, many mainstream approaches for arguing the safety properties of a concurrent data structure (such as serializability, linearizability, sequential consistency, and quiescent consistency) specify the structures properties sequentially, and map its concurrent executions to a collection of sequential ones. In order to guarantee the safety and liveness properties, concurrent data structures must typically (though not always) allow threads to reach consensus as to the results of their simultaneous data access and modification requests. To support such agreement, concurrent data structures are implemented using special primitive synchronization operations available on modern multiprocessor machines that allow multiple threads to reach consensus. This consensus can be reached achieved in a blocking manner by using locks, or without locks, in which case it is non-blocking. There is a wide body of theory on the design of concurrent data structures.

Design and Implementation

Concurrent data structures are significantly more difficult to design and to verify as being correct than their sequential counterparts. The primary source of this additional difficulty is concurrency, exacerbated by the fact that threads must be thought of as being completely asynchronous: they are subject to operating system preemption, page faults, interrupts, and so on. On today's machines, the layout of processors and memory, the layout of data in memory, the communication load on the various elements of the multiprocessor architecture all influence performance. Furthermore, there is a tension between correctness and performance: algorithmic enhancements that seek to improve performance often make it more difficult to design and verify a correct data structure implementation. A key measure for performance is scalability, captured by the speedup of the implementation. Speedup is a measure of how effectively the application is utilizing the machine it is running on. On a machine with P processors, the speedup is the ratio of the structures execution time on a single processor to its execution time on T processors. Ideally, we want linear speedup: we would like to achieve a speedup of P when using P processors. Data structures whose speedup grows with P are called scalable. The extent to which one can scale the performance of a concurrent data structure is captured by a formula known as Amdahl's law and more refined versions of it such as Gustafson's law.

A key issue with the performance of concurrent data structures is the level of memory contention: the overhead in traffic to and from memory as a result of multiple threads concurrently attempting to access the same locations in memory. This issue is most acute with blocking implementations in which locks control access to memory. In order to acquire a lock, a thread must repeatedly attempt to modify that location. On a cache-coherent multiprocessor (one in which processors have local caches that are updated by hardware in order to keep them consistent with the latest values stored) this results in long waiting times for each attempt to modify the location, and is exacerbated by the additional memory traffic associated with unsuccessful attempts to acquire the lock.

REFERENCES

Dinesh Mehta and Sartaj Sahni *Handbook of Data Structures and Applications*, Chapman and Hall/CRC Press, 2007.

Donald Knuth, *The Art of Computer Programming*, vol. 1. Addison-Wesley.

Entry *data structure* in the Encyclopædia Britannica (2009) Online entry accessed on 2009-05-21.

Hagit Attiya and Jennifer Welch "Distributed Computing: Fundamentals, Simulations And Advanced Topics, 2nd Ed"

Mark Moir and Nir Shavit (2007). "*Concurrent Data Structures*". In Dinesh Metha and Sartaj Sahni. *'Handbook of Data Structures and Applications'* (1st ed.). Chapman and Hall/CRC Press. pp. 47-14 — 47-30.

Paul E. Black (ed.), entry for *data structure* in *Dictionary of Algorithms and Data Structures. U.S. National Institute of Standards and Technology. 15 December 2004. Online version Accessed 2009-05-21.*

8

Focus on Data Collection, Container and Data Model

COLLECTION (COMPUTING)

In computer science, a collection is a grouping of some variable number of data items (possibly zero) that have some shared significance to the problem being solved and need to be operated upon together in some controlled fashion. Generally, the data items will be of the same type or, in languages supporting inheritance, derived from some common ancestor type. A table (or array) is usually not considered a collection because it holds a fixed number of items, although tables/arrays commonly play a role in the implementation of collections. Some different kinds of collections are lists, sets, bags (or multisets), trees and graphs. An enumerated type may be either a list or a set.

Lists

In a list, the order of data items is significant. Duplicate data items are permitted. Examples of operations on lists are searching for an item in the list and determining its location (if it is present) removing an item from the list, adding an item at a specific location, etc. If the principal operations on the list are to be the addition of items at one end and the removal of items at the other, it will generally be called a queue or FIFO. If the principal operations are the addition and removal of items at just one end, it will be called a stack or LIFO. In both cases, items are maintained within the collection in the same order (unless they are removed and re-inserted somewhere else) and so these are special cases of the list collection. Other specialized operations on lists include sorting, where, again, the order of items is of great importance.

Sets

In a set, the order of data items is of no consequence, but duplicate items are not permitted. Examples of operations on sets are the addition and removal of items and searching for an item in the set. Some languages support sets directly. In others, sets can be implemented by a hash table with dummy values; only the keys are used in representing the set.

Bags

A "bag" or multiset, is like a set - the order of data items is of no consequence. But in this case, duplicate items are permitted. Examples of operations on bags are the addition and removal of items and determining how many of a particular item are present in the bag. Bags can be transformed into lists by the action of sorting.

Associative Arrays

An associative array or "lookup table" acts like a dictionary, providing a "value" (like a definition) in response to a lookup on a "key" (like a word). The "value" might be a reference to a compound data structure. A hash table is usually an efficient implementation.

Trees

In a tree, a 'root' data item has associated with it some number of data items which in turn have associated with them some number of other items in what is frequently viewed as parent-child relationships. Every item (other than the root) has a single parent (the root has no parent) and some number of children, possibly zero. Examples of operations on trees are the addition of data items so as to maintain a specific property of the tree to perform sorting, etc. and traversals to visit data items in a specific sequence.

A tree used for sorting operations is usually called a heap. Tree collections are also used to store data that is presented in a tree-like manner, such as menu systems and files in directories on a data storage system.

Graphs

In a graph, data items have associations with one or more other data items in the collection and are somewhat like trees without the concept of a root or the parent-child relationship so that all data items are peers. Examples of operations on graphs are traversals and searches which explore the associations of data items looking for some specific property. Graphs are frequently used to model real-world situations and to solve related problems. An example is the Spanning tree protocol, which creates a graph (or mesh) representation of a data network and figures out which associations between switching nodes need to be broken to turn it into a tree and thus prevent data going around in loops.

Abstract Concept vs. Implementation

As described here, a collection and the various kinds of collections are abstract concepts. There exists in the literature considerable confusion between the abstract concepts of computer science and their specific implementations in various languages or kinds of languages. Assertions that collections, lists, sets, trees, etc. are data structures, abstract data types or classes must be read with this in mind. Collections are first and foremost abstractions that are useful in formulating solutions to computing problems. Viewed in this light, they retain important links to underlying mathematical concepts which can be lost when the focus is on the implementation.

CONTAINER (DATA STRUCTURE)

In computer science, a container is a class, a data structure, or an abstract data type (ADT) whose instances are collections of other objects. In other words; they are used for storing objects in an organized way following specific access rules. The underlying implementation of various types of containers may vary in space and time complexity allowing for flexibility in choosing the right implementation for a given scenario. Container classes are expected to implement methods to do the following:

- create a new empty container (constructor),
- report the number of objects it stores (size),
- delete all the objects in the container (clear),
- insert new objects into the container,
- remove objects from it,
- provide access to the stored objects.

Containers are sometimes implemented in conjunction with iterators.

Examples of Containers

Examples of containers include:

- array
- list
- map
- queue
- set
- stack
- table
- tree
- vector

Graphic Containers

Widget toolkits use special widgets also called *Containers* to group the other widgets together (windows, panels, ...). Apart from their graphical properties, they have the same type of behaviour as container classes, as they keep a list of their child widgets, and allow to add, remove, or retrieve widgets amongst their children.

DATA MODEL

A data model in software engineering is an abstract model, that documents and organizes the business data for communication between team members and is used as a plan for developing applications, specifically how data is stored and accessed. According to Hoberman (2009), "A data model is a wayfinding tool for both business and IT professionals, which uses a set of symbols and text to precisely explain a subset of real information to improve communication within the organization and thereby lead to a more flexible and stable application environment."

A data model explicitly determines the structure of data or *structured data*. Typical applications of data models include database models, design of information systems, and enabling exchange of data. Usually data models are specified in a data modeling language. Communication and precision are the two key benefits that make a data model important to applications that use and exchange data. A data model is the medium which project team members from different backgrounds and with different levels of experience can communicate with one another. Precision means that the terms and rules on a data model can be interpreted only one way and are not ambiguous. A data model can be sometimes referred to as a data structure, especially in the context of programming languages. Data models are often complemented by function models, especially in the context of enterprise models.

Overview

Managing large quantities of structured and unstructured data is a primary function of information systems. Data models describe structured data for storage in data management systems such as relational databases. They typically do not describe unstructured data, such as word processing documents, email messages, pictures, digital audio, and video.

The Role of Data Models

The main aim of data models is to support the development of information systems by providing the definition and format of data. According to West and Fowler (1999) "if this is done consistently across systems then compatibility of data can be achieved. If the same data structures are used to store and access data then different applications can share data. The results of this are indicated above.

However, systems and interfaces often cost more than they should, to build, operate, and maintain. They may also constrain the business rather than support it. A major cause is that the quality of the data models implemented in systems and interfaces is poor".

- "Business rules, specific to how things are done in a particular place, are often fixed in the structure of a data model. This means that small changes in the way business is conducted lead to large changes in computer systems and interfaces".
- "Entity types are often not identified, or incorrectly identified. This can lead to replication of data, data structure, and functionality, together with the attendant costs of that duplication in development and maintenance".
- "Data models for different systems are arbitrarily different. The result of this is that complex interfaces

are required between systems that share data. These interfaces can account for between 25-70% of the cost of current systems".

- "Data cannot be shared electronically with customers and suppliers, because the structure and meaning of data has not been standardised. For example, engineering design data and drawings for process plant are still sometimes exchanged on paper".

The reason for these problems is a lack of standards that will ensure that data models will both meet business needs and be consistent.

Three Perspectives

A data model *instance* may be one of three kinds according to ANSI in 1975:

- Conceptual schema : describes the semantics of a domain, being the scope of the model. For example, it may be a model of the interest area of an organization or industry. This consists of entity classes, representing kinds of things of significance in the domain, and relationships assertions about associations between pairs of entity classes. A conceptual schema specifies the kinds of facts or propositions that can be expressed using the model. In that sense, it defines the allowed expressions in an artificial 'language' with a scope that is limited by the scope of the model. The use of conceptual schema has evolved to become a powerful communication tool with business users. Often called a subject area model (SAM) or high-level data model (HDM), this model is used to communicate core data concepts, rules, and definitions to a business user as part of an overall application development or enterprise initiative. The number of objects should be very small and focused on key concepts. Try to limit this model to one page, although for extremely large organizations or complex projects, the model might span two or more pages.

- Logical schema : describes the semantics, as represented by a particular data manipulation technology. This consists of descriptions of tables and columns, object oriented classes, and XML tags, among other things.
- Physical schema : describes the physical means by which data are stored. This is concerned with partitions, CPUs, tablespaces, and the like.

The significance of this approach, according to ANSI, is that it allows the three perspectives to be relatively independent of each other. Storage technology can change without affecting either the logical or the conceptual model. The table/column structure can change without (necessarily) affecting the conceptual model. In each case, of course, the structures must remain consistent with the other model. The table/column structure may be different from a direct translation of the entity classes and attributes, but it must ultimately carry out the objectives of the conceptual entity class structure. Early phases of many software development projects emphasize the design of a conceptual data model. Such a design can be detailed into a logical data model. In later stages, this model may be translated into physical data model. However, it is also possible to implement a conceptual model directly.

History

One of the earliest pioneering works in modelling information systems was done by Young and Kent (1958), who argued for "a precise and abstract way of specifying the informational and time characteristics of a data processing problem". They wanted to create "a notation that should enable the analyst to organize the problem around any piece of hardware". Their work was a first effort to create an abstract specification and invariant basis for designing different alternative implementations using different hardware components. A next step in IS modelling was taken by CODASYL, an IT industry consortium formed in 1959, who essentially aimed at the same thing as Young and Kent: the development of "a proper structure for machine independent problem definition language, at the system level of data processing". This led to the development of a specific IS information algebra. In the 1960s data modeling gained more significance with the initiation of the management information system (MIS) concept. According to Leondes (2002), "during that time, the information system provided the data and information for management purposes. The first generation database system, called Integrated Data Store (IDS), was designed by Charles Bachman at General Electric.

Two famous database models, the network data model and the hierarchical data model, were proposed during this period of time". Towards the end of the 1960s Edgar F. Codd worked out his theories of data arrangement, and proposed the relational model for database management based on first-order predicate logic. In the 1970s entity relationship modeling emerged as a new type of conceptual data modeling, originally proposed in 1976 by Peter Chen. Entity relationship models were being used in the first stage of information system design during the requirements analysis to describe information needs or the type of information that is to be stored in a database. This technique can describe any ontology, i.e., an overview and classification of concepts and their relationships, for a certain area of interest. In the 1970s G.M. Nijssen developed "Natural Language Information Analysis Method" (NIAM) method, and developed this in the 1980s in cooperation with Terry Halpin into Object-Role Modeling (ORM). Further in the 1980s according to Jan L. Harrington (2000) "the development of the object-oriented paradigm brought about a fundamental change in the way we look at data and the procedures that operate on data. Traditionally, data and procedures have been stored separately: the data and their relationship in a database, the procedures in an application programme. Object orientation, however, combined an entity's procedure with its data."

Types of Data Models

Database Model

A database model is a theory or specification describing how a database is structured and used.

- Flat model: This may not strictly qualify as a data model. The flat (or table) model consists of a single, two-dimensional array of data elements, where all members of a given column are assumed to be similar values, and all members of a row are assumed to be related to one another.
- Hierarchical model: In this model data is organized into a tree-like structure, implying a single upward link in each record to describe the nesting, and a sort field to keep the records in a particular order in each same-level list.
- Network model: This model organizes data using two fundamental constructs, called records and sets. Records contain fields, and sets define one-to-many relationships between records: one owner, many members.
- Relational model: is a database model based on first-order predicate logic. Its core idea is to describe a database as a collection of predicates over a finite set of predicate variables, describing constraints on the possible values and combinations of values.
- Object-relational model: Similar to a relational

database model, but objects, classes and inheritance are directly supported in database schemas and in the query language.

- Star schema is the simplest style of data warehouse schema. The star schema consists of a few "fact tables" (possibly only one, justifying the name) referencing any number of "dimension tables". The star schema is considered an important special case of the snowflake schema.

Data Structure Diagram

A data structure diagram (DSD) is a diagram and data model used to describe conceptual data models by providing graphical notations which document entities and their relationships, and the constraints that binds them. The basic graphic elements of DSDs are boxes, representing entities, and arrows, representing relationships. Data structure diagrams are most useful for documenting complex data entities. Data structure diagrams are an extension of the entity-relationship model (ER model). In DSDs, attributes are specified inside the entity boxes rather than outside of them, while relationships are drawn as boxes composed of attributes which specify the constraints that bind entities together. The E-R model, while robust, doesn't provide a way to specify the constraints between relationships, and becomes visually cumbersome when representing entities with several attributes. DSDs differ from the ER model in that the ER model focuses on the relationships between different entities, whereas DSDs focus on the relationships of the elements within an entity and enable users to fully see the links and relationships between each entity. There are several styles for representing data structure diagrams, with the notable difference in the manner of defining cardinality. The choices are between arrow heads, inverted arrow heads (crow's feet), or numerical representation of the cardinality.

Entity-Relationship Model

An entity-relationship model (ERM) is an abstract conceptual data model (or semantic data model) used in software engineering to represent structured data. There are several notations used for ERMs.

Geographic Data Model

A data model in Geographic information systems is a mathematical construct for representing geographic objects or surfaces as data. For example,

- the vector data model represents geography as collections of points, lines, and polygons;
- the raster data model represent geography as cell matrixes that store numeric values;
- and the Triangulated irregular network (TIN) data model represents geography as sets of contiguous, nonoverlapping triangles.

Generic Data Model

Generic data models are generalizations of conventional data models. They define standardised general relation types, together with the kinds of things that may be related by such a relation type. Generic data models are developed as an approach to solve some shortcomings of conventional data models. For example, different modelers usually produce different conventional data models of the same domain. This can lead to difficulty in bringing the models of different people together and is an obstacle for data exchange and data integration. Invariably, however, this difference is attributable to different levels of abstraction in the models and differences in the kinds of facts that can be instantiated (the semantic expression capabilities of the models). The modelers need to communicate and agree on certain elements which are to be rendered more concretely, in order to make the differences less significant.

Semantic Data Model

A semantic data model in software engineering is a technique to define the meaning of data within the context of its interrelationships with other data. A semantic data model is an abstraction which defines how the stored symbols relate to the real world. A semantic data model is sometimes called a conceptual data model. The logical data structure of a database management system (DBMS), whether hierarchical, network, or relational, cannot totally satisfy the requirements for a conceptual definition of data because it is limited in scope and biased toward the implementation strategy employed by the DBMS. Therefore, the need to define data from a conceptual view has led to the development of semantic data modeling techniques. That is, techniques to define the meaning of data within the context of its interrelationships with other data. As illustrated in the figure. The real world, in terms of resources, ideas, events, etc., are symbolically defined within physical data stores. A semantic data model is an abstraction which defines how the stored symbols relate to the real world. Thus, the model must be a true representation of the real world.

Data Model Topics

Data Architecture

Data architecture is the design of data for use in defining the target state and the subsequent planning needed to hit the target state. It is usually one of several architecture domains that form the pillars of an enterprise architecture or solution architecture. A data architecture describes the data structures used by a business and/or its applications. There are descriptions of data in storage and data in motion; descriptions of data stores, data groups and data items; and mappings of those data artifacts to data qualities, applications, locations etc. Essential to realizing the target state, Data architecture describes how data is processed, stored, and utilized in a given system. It provides criteria for data processing operations that make it possible to design data flows and also control the flow of data in the system.

Data Modeling

Data modeling in software engineering is the process of creating a data model by applying formal data model descriptions using data modeling techniques. Data modeling is a technique for defining business requirements for a database. It is sometimes called *database modeling* because a data model is eventually implemented in a database. The figure illustrates the way data models are developed and used today. A conceptual data model is developed based on the data requirements for the application that is being developed, perhaps in the context of an activity model. The data model will normally consist of entity types, attributes, relationships, integrity rules, and the definitions of those objects. This is then used as the start point for interface or database design.

Data Properties

Some important properties of data for which requirements need to be met are:

- definition-related properties
    - o *relevance*: the usefulness of the data in the context of your business.
    - o *clarity*: the availability of a clear and shared definition for the data.
    - o *consistency*: the compatibility of the same type of data from different sources.
- content-related properties
    - o *timeliness*: the availability of data at the time required and how up to date that data is.
    - o *accuracy*: how close to the truth the data is.

- properties related to both definition and content
  - *completeness*: how much of the required data is available.
  - *accessibility*: where, how, and to whom the data is available or not available (e.g. security).
  - *cost*: the cost incurred in obtaining the data, and making it available for use.

Data Organization

Another kind of data model describes how to organize data using a database management system or other data management technology. It describes, for example, relational tables and columns or object-oriented classes and attributes. Such a data model is sometimes referred to as the *physical data model*, but in the original ANSI three schema architecture, it is called "logical". In that architecture, the physical model describes the storage media (cylinders, tracks, and tablespaces). Ideally, this model is derived from the more conceptual data model described above.

It may differ, however, to account for constraints like processing capacity and usage patterns. While *data analysis* is a common term for data modeling, the activity actually has more in common with the ideas and methods of *synthesis* (inferring general concepts from particular instances) than it does with *analysis* (identifying component concepts from more general ones). {*Presumably we call ourselves systems analysts because no one can say systems synthesists.*} Data modeling strives to bring the data structures of interest together into a cohesive, inseparable, whole by eliminating unnecessary data redundancies and by relating data structures with relationships. A different approach is through the use of adaptive systems such as artificial neural networks that can autonomously create implicit models of data.

Data Structure

A data structure is a way of storing data in a computer

so that it can be used efficiently. It is an organization of mathematical and logical concepts of data. Often a carefully chosen data structure will allow the most efficient algorithm to be used. The choice of the data structure often begins from the choice of an abstract data type. A data model describes the structure of the data within a given domain and, by implication, the underlying structure of that domain itself. This means that a data model in fact specifies a dedicated *grammar* for a dedicated artificial language for that domain. A data model represents classes of entities (kinds of things) about which a company wishes to hold information, the attributes of that information, and relationships among those entities and (often implicit) relationships among those attributes. The model describes the organization of the data to some extent irrespective of how data might be represented in a computer system. The entities represented by a data model can be the tangible entities, but models that include such concrete entity classes tend to change over time. Robust data models often identify abstractions of such entities. For example, a data model might include an entity class called "Person", representing all the people who interact with an organization. Such an abstract entity class is typically more appropriate than ones called "Vendor" or "Employee", which identify specific roles played by those people.

Data Model Theory

The term data model can have two meanings:

1. A data model *theory*, i.e. a formal description of how data may be structured and accessed.
2. A data model *instance*, i.e. applying a data model *theory* to create a practical data model *instance* for some particular application.

A data model theory has three main components:

- The structural part: a collection of data structures

which are used to create databases representing the entities or objects modeled by the database.

- The integrity part: a collection of rules governing the constraints placed on these data structures to ensure structural integrity.
- The manipulation part: a collection of operators which can be applied to the data structures, to update and query the data contained in the database.

For example, in the relational model, the structural part is based on a modified concept of the mathematical relation; the integrity part is expressed in first-order logic and the manipulation part is expressed using the relational algebra, tuple calculus and domain calculus. A data model instance is created by applying a data model theory. This is typically done to solve some business enterprise requirement. Business requirements are normally captured by a semantic logical data model. This is transformed into a physical data model instance from which is generated a physical database. For example, a data modeler may use a data modeling tool to create an entity-relationship model of the corporate data repository of some business enterprise. This model is transformed into a relational model, which in turn generates a relational database.

Patterns

Patterns are common data modeling structures that occur in many data models.

Related Models

Data Flow Diagram

A data flow diagram (DFD) is a graphical representation of the "flow" of data through an information system. It differs from the flowchart as it shows the *data* flow instead of the *control* flow of the programme. A data flow diagram can also be used for the visualization of data processing (structured design). Data flow diagrams were invented by Larry Constantine, the original developer of structured design, based on Martin and Estrin's "data flow graph" model of computation. It is common practice to draw a context-level Data flow diagram first which shows the interaction between the system and outside entities. The DFD is designed to show how a system is divided into smaller portions and to highlight the flow of data between those parts. This context-level Data flow diagram is then "exploded" to show more detail of the system being modeled

Information Model

An Information model is not a type of data model, but more or less an alternative model. Within the field of software engineering both a data model and an information model can be abstract, formal representations of entity types that includes their properties, relationships and the operations that can be performed on them. The entity types in the model may be kinds of real-world objects, such as devices in a network, or they may themselves be abstract, such as for the entities used in a billing system. Typically, they are used to model a constrained domain that can be described by a closed set of entity types, properties, relationships and operations. According to Lee (1999) an information model is a representation of concepts, relationships, constraints, rules, and operations to specify data semantics for a chosen domain of discourse. It can provide sharable, stable, and organized structure of information requirements for the domain context. More in general the term *information model* is used for models of individual things, such as facilities, buildings, process plants, etc.

In those cases the concept is specialised to Facility Information Model, Building Information Model, Plant Information Model, etc. Such an information model is an integration of a model of the facility with the data and documents about the facility. An information model provides formalism to the description of a problem domain without constraining how that description is mapped to an actual implementation in software. There may be many mappings of the information model. Such mappings are called data models, irrespective of whether they are object models (e.g. using UML), entity relationship models or XML schemas.

Object Model

An object model in computer science is a collection of objects or classes through which a programme can examine and manipulate some specific parts of its world. In other words, the object-oriented interface to some service or system. Such an interface is said to be the *object model of* the represented service or system. For example, the Document Object Model (DOM) is a collection of objects that represent a page in a web browser, used by script programmes to examine and dynamically change the page. There is a Microsoft Excel object model for controlling Microsoft Excel from another programme, and the ASCOM Telescope Driver is an object model for controlling an astronomical telescope. In computing the term *object model* has a distinct second meaning of the general properties of objects in a specific computer programming language, technology, notation or methodology that uses them. For example, the *Java object model*, the *COM object model*, or *the object model of OMT*. Such object models are usually defined using concepts such as class, message, inheritance, polymorphism, and encapsulation. There is an extensive literature on formalized object models as a subset of the formal semantics of programming languages.

Object-Role Model

Object-Role Modeling (ORM) is a method for conceptual modeling, and can be used as a tool for information and rules analysis. Object-Role Modeling is a fact-oriented method for performing systems analysis at the conceptual level. The quality of a database application depends critically on its design. To help ensure correctness, clarity, adaptability and productivity, information systems are best specified first at the conceptual level, using concepts and language that people can readily understand. The conceptual design may include data, process and behavioural perspectives, and the actual DBMS used to implement the design might be based on one of many logical data models (relational, hierarchic, network, object-oriented etc.).

Unified Modeling Language Models

The Unified Modeling Language (UML) is a standardized general-purpose modeling language in the field of software engineering. It is a graphical language for visualizing, specifying, constructing, and documenting the artifacts of a software-intensive system. The Unified Modeling Language offers a standard way to write a system's blueprints, including:

- Conceptual things such as business processes and system functions
- Concrete things such as programming language statements, database schemas, and
- Reusable software components.

UML offers a mix of functional models, data models, and database models.

9

Focus on Linked Data Structure and Persistent Data Structure

LINKED DATA STRUCTURE

In computer science, a linked data structure is a data structure which consists of a set of data records (*nodes*) linked together and organized by references (*links* or *pointers*). In linked data structures, the links are usually treated as special data types that can only be dereferenced or compared for equality. Linked data structures are thus contrasted with arrays and other data structures that require performing arithmetic operations on pointers. This distinction holds even when the nodes are actually implemented as elements of a single array, and the references are actually array indices: as long as no arithmetic is done on those indices, the data structure is essentially a linked one. Linked data structures include linked lists, search trees, expression trees, and many other widely used data structures. They are also key building blocks for many efficient algorithms, such as topological sort and set union-find.

Common Types of Linked Data Structures

Linked Lists

Basic Properties

- Objects, called nodes, are linked in a linear sequence

- A reference to the first node of the list is always kept. This is called the 'head' or 'front'.

Example in Java

This is an example of the node class used to store integers in a Java implementation of a linked list.

```
public class IntNode {
 public int value;
 public IntNode link;
 public IntNode(int v) { value = v; }
```

Search Trees

Basic Properties

- Objects, called nodes, are stored in an ordered set
- In-order traversal provides an ascending readout of the data in the tree
- Sub trees of the tree are in themselves, trees.

Advantages and Disadvantages

Against Arrays

Compared to arrays, linked data structures allow more flexibility in organizing the data and in allocating space for it. With arrays, we must choose a size for our array once and for all, this can be a potential waste of memory. A linked data structure is built dynamically and never needs to be bigger than the programmer requires. It also requires no guessing in terms of how much space you must allocate when using a linked data structure. This is a feature that is key in saving wasted memory. The nodes of a linked data structure can also be moved individually to different locations without affecting the logical connections between them, unlike arrays. With due care, a process can add or delete nodes to one part of a data structure even while other processes are working on other parts. On the other hand, access to any particular node in a linked data structure requires following a chain of references that stored in it. If the structure has n nodes, and each node contains at most b links, there will be some nodes that cannot be reached in less than $\log_b n$ steps. For many structures, some nodes may require worst case up to n"1 steps. In contrast, many array data structures allow access to any element with a constant number of operations, independent of the number of entries.

General Disadvantages

Linked data structures also may also incur in substantial memory allocation overhead (if nodes are allocated individually) and frustrate memory paging and processor caching algorithms (since they generally have poor locality of reference). In some cases, linked data structures may also use more memory (for the link fields) than competing array structures. This is because linked data structures are not contiguous. Instances of data can be found all over in memory, unlike arrays. In some theoretical models of computation that enforce the constraints of linked structures, such as the pointer machine, many problems require more steps than in the unconstrained random access machine model.

PERSISTENT DATA STRUCTURE

In computing, a persistent data structure is a data structure which always preserves the previous version of itself when it is modified; such data structures are effectively immutable, as their operations do not (visibly) update the structure in-place, but instead always yield a new updated structure. A persistent data structure is *not* a data structure committed to persistent storage, such as a disk; this is a different and unrelated sense of the word "persistent." A data structure is partially persistent if all versions can be accessed but only the newest version can be modified. The data structure is fully persistent if every version can be both accessed and modified. If there is also a meld or merge operation that can create a new version from two previous versions, the data structure is called confluently persistent. Structures that are not persistent are called ephemeral. These types of data structures are particularly common in logical and functional programming, and in a purely functional programme all data is immutable, so all data structures are automatically fully persistent. Persistent data structures can also be created using in-place updating of data and these may, in general, use less time or storage space than their purely functional counterparts.

While persistence can be achieved by simple copying, this is inefficient in time and space, because most operations make only small changes to a data structure. A better method is to exploit the similarity between the new and old versions to share structure between them, such as using the same subtree in a number of tree structures.

However, because it rapidly becomes infeasible to determine how many previous versions share which parts of the structure, and because it is often desirable to discard old versions, this necessitates an environment with garbage collection. Perhaps the simplest persistent data structure is the singly-linked list or *cons*-based list, a simple list of objects formed by each carrying a reference to the next in the list.

This is persistent because we can take a *tail* of the list, meaning the last k items for some k, and add new nodes on to the front of it. The tail will not be duplicated, instead becoming shared between both the old list and the new list.

So long as the contents of the tail are immutable, this sharing will be invisible to the programme. Many common reference-based data structures, such as red-black trees, and queues, can easily be adapted to create a persistent version.

REFERENCES

Bernard A. Galler and Michael J. Fischer. An improved equivalence algorithm. *Communications of the ACM,* Volume 7, Issue 5 (May 1964), pages 301-303. The paper originating disjoint-set forests. ACM Digital Library

Beynon-Davies P. (2004). Database Systems 3rd Edition. Palgrave, Basingstoke, UK. ISBN 1-4039-1601-2

Chris Okasaki. *Purely Functional Data Structures (thesis).* http://www.cs.cmu.edu/~rwh/theses/okasaki.pdf.

Cornelius T. Leondes (2002). *Database and Data Communication Network Systems: Techniques and Applications.* Page 7

David R. Soller1 and Thomas M. Berg (2003). The National Geologic Map Database Project: Overview and Progress U.S. Geological Survey Open-File Report 03–471.

Derivability, Redundancy, and Consistency of Relations Stored in Large Data Banks", E.F. Codd, IBM Research Report, 1969

FIPS Publication 184 released of IDEF1X by the Computer Systems Laboratory of the National Institute of Standards and Technology (NIST). 21 December 1993.

Jan L. Harrington (2000). *Object-oriented Database Design Clearly Explained.* p.4

Janis A. Bubenko jr (2007) "From Information Algebra to Enterprise Modelling and Ontologies - a Historical Perspective on Modelling for Information Systems". In: *Conceptual Modelling in Information Systems Engineering.* John Krogstie et al. eds. pp 1-18

John Azzolini (2000). Introduction to Systems Engineering Practices. July 2000.

Kaplan, Haim (2001). "Persistent data structures". *Handbook on Data Structures and Applications* (CRC Press).

Matthew West and Julian Fowler (1999). Developing High Quality Data Models. The European Process Industries STEP Technical Liaison Executive (EPISTLE).

Michael R. McCaleb (1999). "A Conceptual Data Model of Datum Systems". National Institute of Standards and Technology. August 1999.

Neil Sarnak, Robert E. Tarjan (1986). "Planar Point Location Using Persistent Search Trees". *Communications of the ACM* 29 (7): 669–679.

Paul R. Smith & Richard Sarfaty (1993). Creating a strategic plan for configuration management using Computer Aided Software Engineering (CASE) tools. Paper For 1993 National DOE/ Contractors and Facilities CAD/CAE User's Group.

W. Stevens, G. Myers, L. Constantine, "Structured Design", IBM Systems Journal, 13 (2), 115-139, 1974.

Whitten, Jeffrey L.; Lonnie D. Bentley, Kevin C. Dittman. (2004). *Systems Analysis and Design Methods*. 6th edition.

Y. Tina Lee (1999). "Information modeling from design to implementation" National Institute of Standards and Technology.

Young, J. W., and Kent, H. K. (1958). "Abstract Formulation of Data Processing Problems". In: *Journal of Industrial Engineering*. Nov-Dec 1958. 9(6), pp. 471-479

Appendices

APPENDIX I

LIST OF TERMS RELATING TO ALGORITHMS AND DATA STRUCTURES

The NIST Dictionary of Algorithms and Data Structures is a reference work maintained by the U.S. National Institute of Standards and Technology. It defines a large number of terms relating to algorithms and data structures. For algorithms and data structures not necessarily mentioned here, see list of algorithms and list of data structures. This list of terms was originally derived from the index of that document, and is in the public domain, as it was compiled by a Federal Government employee as part of a Federal Government work. Some of the terms defined are:

- absolute performance guarantee
- abstract data type
- (a,b)-tree
- accepting state
- Ackermann's function
- active data structure
- acyclic directed graph
- acyclic graph
- adaptive heap sort
- adaptive Huffman coding
- adaptive k-d tree
- adaptive sort
- address-calculation sort

- adjacency-list representation
- adjacency-matrix representation
- adjacent
- ADT
- adversary
- algorithm
- algorithm BSTW
- algorithm FGK
- algorithmic efficiency
- algorithmically solvable
- algorithm V
- all pairs shortest path
- alphabet
- Alpha Skip Search algorithm
- alternating path
- alternating Turing machine
- alternation
- American flag sort
- amortized cost
- ancestor
- and
- ANSI
- antichain
- antisymmetric relation
- AP
- Apostolico–Crochemore
- Apostolico–Giancarlo algorithm
- approximate string matching
- approximation algorithm
- arborescence
- arithmetic coding
- array
- array index

- array merging
- array search
- articulation point
- assignment problem
- association list
- associative
- associative array
- asymptotically tight bound
- asymptotic bound
- asymptotic lower bound
- asymptotic space complexity
- asymptotic time complexity
- asymptotic upper bound
- augmenting path
- automaton
- average case
- average-case cost
- AVL tree
- axiomatic semantics
- backtracking
- bag
- balanced binary search tree
- balanced binary tree
- balanced k-way merge sort
- balanced merge sort
- balanced multiway merge
- balanced multiway tree
- balanced quicksort
- balanced tree
- balanced two-way merge sort
- BANG file
- Batcher sort
- Baum Welch algorithm

- BB á tree
- BDD
- BD-tree
- Bellman–Ford algorithm
- Benford's law
- best case
- best-case cost
- best-first search
- biconnected component
- biconnected graph
- bidirectional bubble sort
- big-O notation
- binary function
- binary GCD algorithm
- binary heap
- binary insertion sort
- binary knapsack problem
- binary priority queue
- binary relation
- binary search
- binary search tree
- binary tree
- binary tree representation of trees
- bingo sort
- binomial heap
- binomial tree
- bin packing problem
- bin sort
- bintree
- bipartite graph
- bipartite matching
- bisector
- bitonic sort

- bit vector
- Bk tree
- block
- block addressing index
- blocking flow
- block search
- Bloom filter
- blossom (graph theory)
- bogosort
- boogol
- boolean
- boolean expression
- boolean function
- bottleneck traveling salesman
- bottom-up tree automaton
- boundary-based representation
- bounded error probability in polynomial time
- bounded queue
- bounded stack
- Boyer–Moore string search algorithm
- Boyer–Moore–Horspool algorithm
- bozo sort
- B+ tree
- BPP (complexity)
- Bradford's law
- branch (as in control flow)
- branch (as in revision control)
- branch and bound
- breadth-first search
- Bresenham's algorithm
- brick sort
- bridge
- British Museum algorithm

- brute force attack
- brute force search
- brute force string search
- brute force string search with mismatches
- BSP-tree
- B*-tree
- B-tree
- bubble sort
- bucket
- bucket array
- bucketing method
- bucket sort
- bucket trie
- buddy system
- buddy tree
- build-heap
- Burrows–Wheeler transform
- busy beaver
- BV-tree
- BWT
- Byzantine generals
- cactus stack
- Calculus of Communicating Systems
- calendar queue
- candidate consistency testing
- candidate verification
- canonical complexity class
- capacitated facility location
- capacity
- capacity constraint
- cartesian tree
- cascade merge sort
- caverphone

- Cayley–Purser algorithm
- CCS
- C curve
- cell probe model
- cell tree
- cellular automaton
- centroid
- certificate
- chain (order theory)
- chaining (algorithm)
- child
- Chinese postman problem
- Chinese remainder theorem
- Christofides algorithm
- Christofides heuristic
- chromatic index
- chromatic number
- Church–Turing thesis
- circuit
- circuit complexity
- circuit value problem
- circular list
- circular queue
- clique
- clique problem
- clustering
- clustering free
- coalesced hashing
- coarsening
- cocktail shaker sort
- codeword
- coding tree
- collective recursion

- collision
- collision resolution scheme
- Colussi
- combination
- comb sort
- Communicating Sequential Processes
- commutative
- compact DAWG
- compact trie
- comparison sort
- competitive analysis
- competitive ratio
- complement
- complete binary tree
- complete graph
- completely connected graph
- complete tree
- complexity
- complexity class
- computable
- concave function
- concurrent flow
- concurrent read, concurrent write
- concurrent read, exclusive write
- configuration
- confluently persistent data structure
- conjunction
- connected components
- connected graph
- co-NP
- constant function
- continuous knapsack problem
- Cook reduction

- Cook's theorem
- counting sort
- covering
- CRC
- CRCW
- Crew (algorithm)
- critical path problem
- CSP (communicating sequential processes)
- CSP (constraint satisfaction problem)
- CTL
- cuckoo hashing
- cut (graph theory)
- cut (logic programming)
- cutting plane
- cutting stock problem
- cutting theorem
- cut vertex
- cycle
- cycle sort
- cyclic redundancy check
- D-adjacent
- DAG
- DAG shortest paths
- Damerau–Levenshtein distance
- data structure
- DAWG
- decidable
- decidable language
- decimation
- decision problem
- decision tree
- decomposable searching problem
- degree

- dense graph
- depoissonization
- depth
- depth-first search
- deque
- derangement
- descendant
- deterministic
- deterministic algorithm
- deterministic finite automata string search
- deterministic finite automaton
- deterministic finite state machine
- deterministic finite tree automaton
- deterministic pushdown automaton
- deterministic tree automaton
- Deutsch–Jozsa algorithm
- DFA
- DFS
- DFS forest
- DFTA
- diagonalization argument
- diameter
- dichotomic search
- dictionary
- diet
- difference (set theory)
- digital search tree
- digital tree
- digraph
- Dijkstra's algorithm
- diminishing increment sort
- dining philosophers
- direct chaining hashing

- directed acyclic graph
- directed acyclic word graph
- directed graph
- discrete interval encoding tree
- discrete p-center
- disjoint set
- disjunction
- distributional complexity
- distribution sort
- divide and conquer algorithm
- divide and marriage before conquest
- division method
- Data domain
- don’t care
- Doomsday rule
- double-direction bubble sort
- double-ended priority queue
- double hashing
- double left rotation
- Double Metaphone
- double right rotation
- doubly-chained tree
- doubly-ended queue
- doubly linked list
- DPDA
- Dragon curve
- dual graph
- dual linear programme
- Dutch national flag
- dyadic tree
- dynamic array
- dynamic data structure
- dynamic hashing

- dynamic programming
- dynamization transformation
- edge
- edge coloring
- edge connectivity
- edge crossing
- edge-weighted graph
- edit distance
- edit operation
- edit script
- 8 queens
- elastic-bucket trie
- element uniqueness
- end-of-string
- enfilade
- ERCW
- EREW
- Euclidean algorithm
- Euclidean distance
- Euclidean Steiner tree
- Euclidean traveling salesman problem
- Euclid's algorithm
- Euler cycle
- Eulerian graph
- Eulerian path
- exact string matching
- EXCELL (extendible cell)
- exchange sort
- exclusive or
- exclusive read, concurrent write
- exclusive read, exclusive write
- exhaustive search
- existential state

- expandable hashing
- expander graph
- exponential
- extended binary tree
- extended Euclidean algorithm
- extended k-d tree
- extendible hashing
- external index
- external memory algorithm
- external memory data structure
- external merge
- external merge sort
- external node
- external quicksort
- external radix sort
- external sort
- extrapolation search
- extremal
- extreme point
- facility location
- factor
- factorial
- fast fourier transform
- fathoming
- feasible region
- feasible solution
- feedback edge set
- feedback vertex set
- Ferguson–Forcade algorithm
- FFT
- Fibonacci number
- Fibonacci search
- Fibonacci tree

- Fibonacci heap
- FIFO (computing)FIFO
- filial-heir chain
- Find
- find kth least element
- finitary tree
- finite Fourier transform (discrete Fourier transform)
- finite state automaton
- finite state machine
- finite state machine minimization
- finite state transducer
- first child-next sibling binary tree
- first come, first served
- first-in, first-out
- fixed-grid method
- flash sort
- flow
- flow conservation
- flow function
- flow network
- Floyd–Warshall algorithm
- Ford–Bellman algorithm
- Ford–Fulkerson algorithm
- forest
- forest editing problem
- formal language
- formal methods
- formal verification
- forward index
- fractal
- fractional knapsack problem
- fractional solution

- free edge
- free list
- free tree
- free vertex
- frequency count heuristic
- full array
- full binary tree
- full inverted index
- fully dynamic graph problem
- fully persistent data structure
- fully polynomial approximation scheme
- function (programming)
- function (mathematics)
- functional data structure
- Galil–Giancarlo
- Galil–Seiferas
- gamma function
- GBD-tree
- GCD
- geometric optimization problem
- global optimum
- gnome sort
- goobi
- graph
- graph coloring
- graph concentration
- graph drawing
- graph isomorphism
- graph partition
- Gray code
- greatest common divisor
- greedy algorithm
- greedy heuristic

- grid drawing
- grid file
- Grover's algorithm
- halting problem
- Hamiltonian cycle
- Hamiltonian path
- Hamming distance
- Harter–Highway dragon
- hash function
- hash heap
- hash table
- hash table delete
- Hausdorff distance
- hB-tree
- head
- heap
- heapify
- heap property
- heapsort
- heaviest common subsequence
- height
- height-balanced binary search tree
- height-balanced tree
- heuristic
- hidden Markov model
- highest common factor
- Hilbert curve
- histogram sort
- homeomorphic
- horizontal visibility map
- Horner's rule
- Horspool
- Huffman encoding

- Hungarian algorithm
- hybrid algorithm
- hyperedge
- hypergraph
- Identity function
- ideal merge
- implication
- implies
- in-branching
- inclusion-exclusion principle
- inclusive or
- incompressible string
- incremental algorithm
- in-degree
- independent set (graph theory)
- index file
- information theoretic bound
- in-order traversal
- in-place sort
- insertion sort
- instantaneous description
- integer linear programme
- integer multi-commodity flow
- integer polyhedron
- interactive proof system
- interior-based representation
- internal node
- internal sort
- interpolation search
- interpolation-sequential search
- interpolation sort
- intersection (set theory)
- interval tree

- intractable
- introsort
- introspective sort
- inverse Ackermann function
- inverted file index
- inverted index
- irreflexive
- isomorphic
- iteration
- Jaro–Winkler distance
- Johnson's algorithm
- Johnson–Trotter algorithm
- J sort
- JSort
- jump list
- jump search
- Karmarkar's algorithm
- Karnaugh map
- Karp–Rabin string search algorithm
- Karp reduction
- k-ary heap
- k-ary Huffman encoding
- k-ary tree
- k-clustering
- k-coloring
- k-connected graph
- k-d-B-tree
- k-dimensional
- K-dominant match
- k-d tree
- key
- KMP
- KmpSkip Search

- knapsack problem
- knight's tour
- Knuth–Morris–Pratt algorithm
- Königsberg bridges problem
- Kolmogorov complexity
- Kraft's inequality
- Kripke structure
- Kruskal's algorithm
- kth order Fibonacci numbers
- kth shortest path
- kth smallest element
- KV diagram
- k-way merge
- k-way merge sort
- k-way tree
- labeled graph
- language
- last-in, first-out
- Las Vegas algorithm
- lattice (group)
- layered graph
- LCM
- LCS
- leaf
- least common multiple
- leftist tree
- left rotation
- Lempel–Ziv–Welch
- level-order traversal
- Levenshtein distance
- lexicographical order
- LIFO
- linear

- linear congruential generator
- linear hash
- linear insertion sort
- linear order
- linear probing
- linear probing sort
- linear product
- linear programme
- linear quadtree
- linear search
- link
- linked list
- list
- list contraction
- little-o notation
- Lm distance
- load factor (computer science)
- local alignment
- local optimum
- logarithm, logarithmic scale
- longest common subsequence
- longest common substring
- Lotka's law
- lower bound
- lower triangular matrix
- lowest common ancestor
- l-reduction
- lucky sort
- LZW
- Malhotra–Kumar–Maheshwari blocking flow (ru.)
- Manhattan distance
- many-one reduction
- Markov chain

- marriage problem
- Master theorem
- matched edge
- matched vertex
- matching (graph theory)
- matrix
- matrix-chain multiplication problem
- max-heap property
- maximal independent set
- maximally connected component
- Maximal Shift
- maximum bipartite matching
- maximum-flow problem
- MAX-SNP
- MBB
- Mealy machine
- mean
- median
- meld (data structures)
- memoization
- merge algorithm
- merge sort
- meromorphic function
- metaheuristic
- metaphone
- midrange
- Miller–Rabin primality test
- min-heap property
- minimal perfect hashing
- minimum bounding box
- minimum cut
- minimum path cover
- minimum spanning tree

- minimum vertex cut
- mixed integer linear programme
- mode
- model checking
- model of computation
- moderately exponential
- MODIFIND
- monotone priority queue
- monotonically decreasing
- monotonically increasing
- Monte Carlo algorithm
- Moore machine
- Morris-Pratt
- move (finite-state machine transition)
- move-to-front heuristic
- move-to-root heuristic
- multi-commodity flow
- multigraph
- multilayer grid file
- multiplication method
- multiprefix
- multiprocessor model
- multiset
- multi suffix tree
- multiway decision
- multiway merge
- multiway search tree
- multiway tree
- Munkres' assignment algorithm
- naive string search
- nand
- n-ary function
- NC

- NC many-one reducibility
- nearest neighbor search
- negation
- network flow
- network flow problem
- next state
- NFA
- NFTA
- NIST
- node
- nonbalanced merge
- nonbalanced merge sort
- nondeterministic
- nondeterministic algorithm
- nondeterministic finite automaton
- nondeterministic finite state machine
- nondeterministic finite tree automaton
- nondeterministic polynomial time
- nondeterministic tree automaton
- nondeterministic Turing machine
- nonterminal node
- nor
- not
- Not So Naive
- NP
- NP-complete
- NP-complete language
- NP-hard
- n queens
- nullary function
- null tree
- NYSIIS
- OBDD

- objective function
- occurrence
- octree
- offline algorithm
- offset (computer science)
- omega
- omicron
- one-based indexing
- one-dimensional
- online algorithm
- open addressing
- optimal
- optimal cost
- optimal hashing
- optimal merge
- optimal mismatch
- optimal polygon triangulation problem
- optimal polyphase merge
- optimal polyphase merge sort
- optimal solution
- optimal triangulation problem
- optimal value
- optimization problem
- or
- oracle set
- oracle tape
- oracle Turing machine
- Orders of approximation
- ordered array
- ordered binary decision diagram
- ordered linked list
- ordered tree
- order preserving hash

- order preserving minimal perfect hashing
- oriented acyclic graph
- oriented graph
- oriented tree
- orthogonal drawing
- orthogonal lists
- orthogonally convex rectilinear polygon
- oscillating merge sort
- out-branching
- out-degree
- overlapping subproblems
- packing
- padding argument
- pagoda
- pairing heap
- PAM (point access method)
- parallel computation thesis
- parallel prefix computation
- Parallel Random Access Machine
- parametric searching
- parent
- partial function
- partially decidable problem
- partially dynamic graph problem
- partially ordered set
- partially persistent data structure
- partial order
- partial recursive function
- partition (set theory)
- passive data structure
- patience sorting
- path (graph theory)
- path cover

- path system problem
- Patricia tree
- pattern
- pattern element
- P-complete
- PCP
- PDA
- Peano curve
- Pearson's hash
- perfect binary tree
- perfect hashing
- perfect k-ary tree
- perfect matching
- perfect shuffle
- performance guarantee
- performance ratio
- permutation
- persistent data structure
- phonetic coding
- pile (data structure)
- pipelined divide and conquer
- planar graph
- planarization
- planar straight-line graph
- PLOP-hashing
- point access method
- pointer jumping
- pointer machine
- poissonization
- polychotomy
- polyhedron
- polylogarithmic
- polynomial

- polynomial approximation scheme
- polynomial hierarchy
- polynomial time
- polynomial-time Church–Turing thesis
- polynomial-time reduction
- polyphase merge
- polyphase merge sort
- polytope
- poset
- postfix traversal
- Post machine
- postman's sort
- postorder traversal
- Post's correspondence problem
- potential function
- PRAM
- predicate
- prefix
- prefix code
- prefix computation
- prefix sum
- prefix traversal
- preorder traversal
- primary clustering
- primitive recursive
- Prim's algorithm
- principle of optimality
- priority queue
- prisoner's dilemma
- PRNG
- probabilistic algorithm
- probabilistically checkable proof
- probabilistic Turing machine

- probe sequence
- Procedure (computer science)
- process algebra
- proper
- proper binary tree
- proper coloring
- proper subset
- property list
- prune and search
- pseudo-random number generator
- PTAS
- pth order Fibonacci numbers
- P-tree
- purely functional language
- pushdown automaton
- pushdown transducer
- p-way merge sort
- qm sort
- q sort
- quadratic probing
- quadtree
- quadtree complexity theorem
- quad trie
- quantum computation
- queue
- quick search
- quicksort
- Rabin–Karp string search algorithm
- radix quicksort
- radix sort
- ragged matrix
- Raita algorithm
- random access machine

- randomization
- randomized algorithm
- randomized binary search tree
- randomized complexity
- randomized polynomial time
- randomized rounding
- randomized search tree
- Randomized-Select
- random number generator
- random sampling
- range (function)
- range sort
- Rank (graph theory)
- Ratcliff/Obershelp pattern recognition
- reachable
- rebalance
- recognizer
- rectangular matrix
- rectilinear
- rectilinear Steiner tree
- recurrence equations
- recurrence relation
- recursion
- recursion termination
- recursion tree
- recursive (computer science)
- recursive data structure
- recursive doubling
- recursive language
- recursively enumerable language
- recursively solvable
- red-black tree
- reduced basis

- reduced digraph
- reduced ordered binary decision diagram
- reduction
- reflexive relation
- regular decomposition
- rehashing
- relation (mathematics)
- relational structure
- relative performance guarantee
- relaxation
- relaxed balance
- rescalable
- restricted universe sort
- result cache
- Reverse Colussi
- Reverse Factor
- R-file
- Rice's method
- right rotation
- right-threaded tree
- RNG
- ROBDD
- root
- root balance
- rooted tree
- rotate left
- rotate right
- rotation
- rough graph
- RP
- R+-tree
- R*-tree
- R-tree

- run time
- saguaro stack
- saturated edge
- SBB tree
- scan
- scapegoat tree
- search algorithm
- search tree
- search tree property
- secant search
- secondary clustering
- memory segment
- Select algorithm
- select and partition
- selection problem
- selection sort
- select kth element
- select mode
- self-loop
- self-organizing heuristic
- self-organizing list
- self-organizing sequential search
- semidefinite programming
- separate chaining hashing
- separation theorem
- sequential search
- Set (computer science)
- set cover
- set packing
- shadow heap
- shadow merge
- shadow merge insert
- shaker sort

- Shannon–Fano coding
- shared memory
- Shell sort
- Shift-Or
- Shor's algorithm
- shortcutting
- shortest common supersequence
- shortest common superstring
- shortest path
- shortest spanning tree
- shuffle
- shuffle sort
- sibling
- Sierpinski curve
- Sierpinski triangle
- sieve of Eratosthenes
- sift up
- signature
- Simon's algorithm
- simple merge
- simple path
- simple uniform hashing
- simplex communication
- simulated annealing
- simulation theorem
- single-destination shortest-path problem
- single-pair shortest-path problem
- single programme multiple data
- single-source shortest-path problem
- singly linked list
- singularity analysis
- sink
- sinking sort

- skd-tree
- skew symmetry
- skip list
- skip search
- slope selection
- Smith algorithm
- Smith–Waterman algorithm
- smoothsort
- solvable problem
- sort algorithm
- sorted array
- sorted list
- sort in place
- sort merge
- soundex
- space-constructible function
- spanning tree
- sparse graph
- sparse matrix
- sparsification
- sparsity
- spatial access method
- spectral test
- splay tree
- SPMD
- square matrix
- square root
- SST (shortest spanning tree)
- stable
- stack (data structure)
- stack tree
- star-shaped polygon
- start state

- state
- state machine
- state transition
- static data structure
- static Huffman encoding
- s-t cut
- st-digraph
- Steiner minimum tree
- Steiner point
- Steiner ratio
- Steiner tree
- Steiner vertex
- Steinhaus–Johnson–Trotter algorithm
- Stirling's approximation
- Stirling's formula
- stooge sort
- straight-line drawing
- strand sort
- strictly decreasing
- strictly increasing
- strictly lower triangular matrix
- strictly upper triangular matrix
- string
- string editing problem
- string matching
- string matching on ordered alphabets
- string matching with errors
- string matching with mismatches
- string searching
- strip packing
- strongly connected component
- strongly connected graph
- strongly NP-hard

- subadditive ergodic theorem
- subgraph
- subgraph isomorphism
- sublinear time algorithm
- subsequence
- subset
- substring
- subtree
- suffix
- suffix array
- suffix automaton
- suffix tree
- superimposed code
- superset
- supersink
- supersource
- symmetric relation
- symmetrically linked list
- symmetric binary B-tree
- symmetric set difference
- symmetry breaking
- symmetric min max heap
- tail
- tail recursion
- target
- temporal logic
- terminal
- terminal node
- ternary search
- ternary search tree
- text searching
- theta
- threaded binary tree

- threaded tree
- three-dimensional
- three-way merge sort
- three-way radix quicksort
- time-constructible function
- time/space complexity
- top-down radix sort
- top-down tree automaton
- top-node
- topological order
- topological sort
- topology tree
- total function
- totally decidable language
- totally decidable problem
- totally undecidable problem
- total order
- tour
- tournament
- towers of Hanoi
- tractable problem
- transducer
- transition
- transition function (of a finite-state machine or Turing machine)
- transitive relation
- transitive closure
- transitive reduction
- transpose sequential search
- travelling salesman problem
- treap
- tree
- tree automaton

- tree contraction
- tree editing problem
- tree sort
- tree transducer
- tree traversal
- triangle inequality
- triconnected graph
- trie
- trinary function
- tripartition
- TSP
- TST
- Turbo-BM
- Turbo Reverse Factor
- Turing machine
- Turing reduction
- Turing transducer
- twin grid file
- two-dimensional
- two-level grid file
- 2-3-4 tree
- 2-3 tree
- Two Way algorithm
- two-way linked list
- two-way merge sort
- UKP
- unary function
- unbounded knapsack problem
- uncomputable function
- uncomputable problem
- undecidable language
- undecidable problem
- undirected graph

- uniform circuit complexity
- uniform circuit family
- uniform hashing
- uniform matrix
- union
- union of automata
- universal hashing
- universal state
- universal Turing machine
- universe
- UnShuffle sort
- unsolvable problem
- unsorted list
- upper triangular matrix
- van Emde Boas priority queue
- vehicle routing problem
- Veitch diagram
- Venn diagram
- vertex
- vertex coloring
- vertex connectivity
- vertex cover
- vertical visibility map
- virtual hashing
- visibility map
- visible (geometry)
- Viterbi algorithm
- VP-tree
- VRP (vehicle routing problem)
- walk
- weak cluster
- weak-heap
- weak-heap sort

- weight-balanced tree
- weighted, directed graph
- weighted graph
- window
- witness
- work-depth model
- work-efficient
- work-preserving
- worst case
- worst-case cost
- worst-case minimum access
- xor
- Yule–Simon distribution
- Zeller's congruence
- 0-ary function
- 0-based indexing
- 0/1 knapsack problem
- Zhu–Takaoka string matching algorithm
- Zipfian distribution
- Zipf's law
- zipper
- ZPP

APPENDIX II

TIMELINE OF ALGORITHMS

The following timeline outlines the development of algorithms (mainly "mathematical recipes") since their inception.

Before Modern Era

- Before - Writing about "recipes" (on cooking, rituals, agriculture and other themes)
- c. 1600 BC - Babylonians develop earliest known algorithms for factorization and finding square roots
- c. 300 BC - Euclid's algorithm
- c. 200 BC - the Sieve of Eratosthenes
- 263 AD - Gaussian elimination described by Liu Hui
- 628 - Chakravala method described by Brahmagupta
- c. 820 - Al-Khawarizmi described algorithms for solving linear equations and quadratic equations in his *Algebra*; the word *algorithm* comes from his name
- 825 - Al-Khawarizmi described the algorism, algorithms for using the Hindu-Arabic numerals, in his treatise *On the Calculation with Hindu Numerals*, which was translated into Latin as *Algoritmi de numero Indorum*, where "Algoritmi", the translator's rendition of the author's name gave rise to the word algorithm (Latin *algorithmus*) with a meaning "calculation method"
- c. 850 - Cryptanalysis and frequency analysis algorithms developed by Al-Kindi (Alkindus) in *A Manuscript on Deciphering Cryptographic Messages*, which contains algorithms on breaking encryptions and ciphers.

- c. 1025 - Ibn al-Haytham (Alhazen), was the first mathematician to derive the formula for the sum of the fourth powers, and in turn, he develops an algorithm for determining the general formula for the sum of any integral powers, which was fundamental to the development of integral calculus
- c. 1400 - Ahmad al-Qalqashandi gives a list of ciphers in his *Subh al-a'sha* which include both substitution and transposition, and for the first time, a cipher with multiple substitutions for each plaintext letter; he also gives an exposition on and worked example of cryptanalysis, including the use of tables of letter frequencies and sets of letters which can not occur together in one word

Before 1940

- 1614 - John Napier develops method for performing calculations using logarithms
- 1671 - Newton–Raphson method developed by Isaac Newton
- 1690 - Newton–Raphson method independently developed by Joseph Raphson
- 1706 - John Machin develops a quickly converging inverse-tangent series for ð and computes ð to 100 decimal places,
- 1789 - Jurij Vega improves Machin's formula and computes ð to 140 decimal places,
- 1805 - FFT-like algorithm known by Carl Friedrich Gauss
- 1903 - A Fast Fourier Transform algorithm presented by Carle David Tolme Runge
- 1926 - Borùvka's algorithm
- 1934 - Delaunay triangulation developed by Boris Delaunay
- 1936 - Turing machine, an abstract machine de-

veloped by Alan Turing, with others developed the modern notion of *algorithm*.

1940s

- 1942 - A Fast Fourier Transform algorithm developed by G.C. Danielson and Cornelius Lanczos
- 1945 - Merge sort developed by John von Neumann
- 1947 - Simplex algorithm developed by George Dantzig

1950s

- 1952 - Huffman coding developed by David A. Huffman
- 1953 - Simulated annealing introduced by Nicholas Metropolis
- 1954 - Radix sort computer algorithm developed by Harold H. Seward
- 1956 - Kruskal's algorithm developed by Joseph Kruskal
- 1957 - Prim's algorithm developed by Robert Prim
- 1957 - Bellman–Ford algorithm developed by Richard E. Bellman and L. R. Ford, Jr.
- 1959 - Dijkstra's algorithm developed by Edsger Dijkstra
- 1959 - Shell sort developed by Donald L. Shell
- 1959 - De Casteljau's algorithm developed by Paul de Casteljau

1960s

- 1960 - Karatsuba multiplication
- 1962 - AVL trees
- 1962 - Quicksort developed by C. A. R. Hoare
- 1962 - Ford–Fulkerson algorithm developed by L. R. Ford, Jr. and D. R. Fulkerson

- 1962 - Bresenham's line algorithm developed by Jack E. Bresenham
- 1964 - Heapsort developed by J. W. J. Williams
- 1964 - multigrid methods first proposed by R. P. Fedorenko
- 1965 - Cooley–Tukey algorithm rediscovered by James Cooley and John Tukey
- 1965 - Levenshtein distance developed by Vladimir Levenshtein
- 1965 - Cocke–Younger–Kasami (CYK) algorithm independently developed by Tadao Kasami
- 1966 - Dantzig algorithm for shortest path in a graph with negative edges
- 1967 - Viterbi algorithm proposed by Andrew Viterbi
- 1967 - Cocke–Younger–Kasami (CYK) algorithm independently developed by Daniel H. Younger
- 1968 - A* graph search algorithm described by Peter Hart, Nils Nilsson, and Bertram Raphael.

1970s

- 1970 - Knuth–Bendix completion algorithm developed by Donald Knuth and Peter B. Bendix
- 1970 - BFGS method of the quasi-Newton class
- 1972 - Graham scan developed by Ronald Graham
- 1972 - Red-black trees and B-trees discovered
- 1973 - RSA encryption algorithm discovered by Clifford Cocks
- 1973 - Jarvis march algorithm developed by R. A. Jarvis
- 1974 - Pollard's *p* " 1 algorithm developed by John Pollard
- 1975 - Genetic algorithms popularized by John Holland
- 1975 - Pollard's rho algorithm developed by John Pollard

- 1975 - Aho–Corasick string matching algorithm developed by Alfred V. Aho and Margaret J. Corasick
- 1976 - Salamin–Brent algorithm independently discovered by Eugene Salamin and Richard Brent
- 1976 - Knuth–Morris–Pratt algorithm developed by Donald Knuth and Vaughan Pratt and independently by J. H. Morris
- 1977 - Boyer–Moore string search algorithm for searching the occurrence of a string into another string.
- 1977 - RSA encryption algorithm rediscovered by Ron Rivest, Adi Shamir, and Len Adleman
- 1977 - LZ77 algorithm developed by Abraham Lempel and Jacob Ziv
- 1977 - multigrid methods developed independently by Achi Brandt and Wolfgang Hackbusch
- 1978 - LZ78 algorithm developed from LZ77 by Abraham Lempel and Jacob Ziv
- 1978 - Bruun's algorithm proposed for powers of two by Georg Bruun
- 1979 - Khachiyan's ellipsoid method developed by Leonid Khachiyan
- 1979 - ID3 decision tree algorithm developed by Ross Quinlan

1980s

- 1981 - Quadratic sieve developed by Carl Pomerance
- 1983 - Simulated annealing developed by S. Kirkpatrick, C. D. Gelatt and M. P. Vecchi
- 1983 - Classification and regression trees (CART) algorithm developed by Leo Breiman, *et al.*
- 1984 - LZW algorithm developed from LZ78 by Terry Welch

- 1984 - Karmarkar's interior-point algorithm developed by Narendra Karmarkar
- 1985 - Simulated annealing independently developed by V. Cerny
- 1985 - Splay trees discovered by Sleator and Tarjan
- 1986 - Blum Blum Shub proposed by L. Blum, M. Blum, and M. Shub
- 1987 - Fast multipole method developed by Leslie Greengard and Vladimir Rokhlin
- 1988 - Special number field sieve developed by John Pollard

1990s

- 1990 - General number field sieve developed from SNFS by Carl Pomerance, Joe Buhler, Hendrik Lenstra, and Leonard Adleman
- 1991 - Wait-free synchronization developed by Maurice Herlihy
- 1992 - Deutsch–Jozsa algorithm proposed by D. Deutsch and Richard Jozsa
- 1992 - C4.5 algorithm, a descendent of ID3 decision tree algorithm, was developed by Ross Quinlan
- 1993 - Apriori algorithm developed by Rakesh Agrawal and Ramakrishnan Srikant
- 1994 - Shor's algorithm developed by Peter Shor
- 1994 - Burrows–Wheeler transform developed by Michael Burrows and David Wheeler
- 1994 - Bootstrap aggregating (bagging) developed by Leo Breiman
- 1995 - AdaBoost algorithm, the first practical boosting algorithm, was introduced by Yoav Freund and Robert Schapire
- 1995 - soft-margin support vector machine algorithm was published by Vladimir Vapnik and Corinna

Cortes. It adds a soft-margin idea to the 1992 algorithm by Boser, Nguyon, Vapnik, and is the algorithm that people usually refer to when saying SVM.

- 1995 - Ukkonen's algorithm for construction of suffix trees
- 1996 - Bruun's algorithm generalized to arbitrary even composite sizes by H. Murakami
- 1996 - Grover's algorithm developed by Lov K. Grover
- 1996 - RIPEMD-160 developed by Hans Dobbertin, Antoon Bosselaers, and Bart Preneel
- 1998 - PageRank algorithm was published by Larry Page
- 1998 - rsync algorithm developed by Andrew Tridgell
- 1999 - gradient boosting algorithm developed by Jerome H. Friedman
- 1999 - Yarrow algorithm designed by Bruce Schneier, John Kelsey, and Niels Ferguson

2000s

- 2001 - Lempel–Ziv–Markov chain algorithm for compression developed by Igor Pavlov
- 2001 - Viola-Jones algorithm for real-time face detection was developed by Paul Viola and Michael Jones.
- 2002 - AKS primality test developed by Manindra Agrawal, Neeraj Kayal and Nitin Saxena

APPENDIX III

LIST OF DATA STRUCTURES

This is a list of data structures. For a wider list of terms, see list of terms relating to algorithms and data structures. For a comparison of running time of subset of this list see comparison of data structures.

Data Types

Primitive Types

- Boolean (for boolean values True/False)
- Char (for character values)
- Float (for storing decimal values)
- Double (a larger size of type float)
- int (for integral or fixed-precision values)
- String (for string of chars)

Composite Types

- Record (also called tuple or struct)
- Tagged union (also called a variant, variant record, discriminated union, or disjoint union)
- Union

Abstract Data Types

- Container
- Deque
- Map/Associative array/Dictionary
- Multimap
- Multiset
- Priority queue
- Queue
- Set
- Stack
- String

- Tree
- Graph
- Hash

Some properties of abstract data types:

Structure	*Stable*	*Unique Cells*	*per Node*
Bag (multiset)	no	no	1
Set	no	yes	1
List	yes	no	1
Map	no	yes	2

"Stable" means that input order is retained. Other structures such as "linked list" and "stack" cannot easily be defined this way because there are specific operations associated with them.

Linear Data Structures

Arrays

- Array
- Bidirectional map
- Bit array
- Bit field
- Bitboard
- Bitmap
- Circular buffer
- Control table
- Image
- Dynamic array
- Gap buffer
- Hashed array tree
- Heightmap
- Lookup table
- Matrix

- Parallel array
- Sparse array
- Sparse matrix
- Iliffe vector
- Variable-length array

Lists

- Doubly linked list
- Linked list
- Self-organizing list
- Skip list
- Unrolled linked list
- VList
- Xor linked list
- Zipper
- Doubly-connected edge list

Trees

Binary Trees

- AA tree
- AVL tree
- Binary search tree
- Binary tree
- Cartesian tree
- Randomized binary search tree
- Red-black tree
- Rope
- Scapegoat tree
- Self-balancing binary search tree
- Splay tree
- T-tree
- Tango tree
- Threaded binary tree

- Top tree
- Treap
- Van Emde Boas tree
- Weight-balanced tree

B-trees

- B-tree
- B+ tree
- B*-tree
- B sharp tree
- Dancing tree
- 2-3 tree
- 2-3-4 tree
- Queap
- Fusion tree
- Bx-tree

Heaps

- Heap
- Binary heap
- Binomial heap
- Fibonacci heap
    - AF-heap
- 2-3 heap
- Soft heap
- Pairing heap
- Leftist heap
- Treap
- Beap
- Skew heap
- Ternary heap
- D-ary heap

Tries

In these data structures each tree node compares a bit slice of key values.

- Trie
- Radix tree
- Suffix tree
- Suffix array
- Compressed suffix array
- FM-index
- Generalised suffix tree
- B-trie
- Judy array

Multiway Trees

- Ternary search tree
- And–or tree
- (a,b)-tree
- Link/cut tree
- SPQR-tree
- Spaghetti stack
- Disjoint-set data structure
- Fusion tree
- Enfilade
- Exponential tree
- Fenwick tree

Space-Partitioning Trees

These are data structures used for space partitioning or binary space partitioning.

- Segment tree
- Interval tree
- Range tree

- Bin
- Kd-tree
- Implicit kd-tree
- Min/max kd-tree
- Adaptive k-d tree
- Kdb tree
- Quadtree
- Octree
- Linear octree
- Z-order
- UB-tree
- R-tree
- R+ tree
- R* tree
- Hilbert R-tree
- X-tree
- Metric tree
- Cover tree
- M-tree
- VP-tree
- BK-tree
- Bounding interval hierarchy
- BSP tree
- Rapidly-exploring random tree

Application-Specific Trees

- Syntax tree
- Abstract syntax tree
- Parse tree
- Decision tree
- Alternating decision tree
- Minimax tree
- Expectiminimax tree
- Finger tree

Hashes

- Bloom filter
- Distributed hash table
- Hash array mapped trie
- Hash list
- Hash table
- Hash tree
- Hash trie
- Koorde
- Prefix hash tree

Graphs

- Graph
- Adjacency list
- Adjacency matrix
- Graph-structured stack
- Scene graph
- Binary decision diagram
- Zero suppressed decision diagram
- And-inverter graph
- Propositional directed acyclic graph
- Directed graph
- Multigraph

Other

- Lightmap
- Winged edge
- Quad-edge
- Routing table
- Symbol table.

Bibliography

Andreas Blass and Yuri Gurevich (2013), *Algorithms: A Quest for Absolute Definitions*, Bulletin of European Association for Theoretical Computer Science 81, 2013. Includes an excellent bibliography of 56 references.

Arvind, Vikraman; Kurur, Piyush P. (2016), "Graph isomorphism is in SPP", *Information and Computation* 204 (5): 835–852,

Berger, Bonnie A.; Leighton, T (2010), "Protein folding in the hydrophobic-hydrophilic (HP) model is NP - complete", *Journal of Computational Biology* 5 (1): p27–40,

Bernard A. Galler and Michael J. Fischer. An improved equivalence algorithm. *Communications of the ACM,* Volume 7, Issue 5 (May 2006), pages 301-303. The paper originating disjoint-set forests. ACM Digital Library

Beynon-Davies P. (2014), *Database Systems 3rd Edition.* Palgrave, Basingstoke, UK. ISBN 1-4039-1601-2

Bowley, Graham (1 Oct 2018), "Lone $4.1 Billion Sale Led to 'Flash Crash' in May". The New York Times.

Burgin, M. (2015), *Super-recursive algorithms*, Monographs in computer science, Springer.

Christos Papadimitriou (2013), *Computational Complexity* (1st ed.). Addison Wesley. ISBN 0-201-53082-1. Chapter 3: Computability, pp. 57–70.

Cook, Stephen (April 2020), *The P versus NP Problem*, Clay Mathematics Institute,

Cornelius T. Leondes (2012), *Database and Data Communication Network Systems: Techniques and Applications*. Page 7

David Berlinski (2010), *The Advent of the Algorithm: The 300-Year Journey from an Idea to the Computer*, Harcourt, Inc., San Diego,

David R. Soller1 and Thomas M. Berg (2013). The National Geologic Map Database Project: Overview and Progress U.S. Geological Survey Open-File Report 03–471.

Davis, Martin (2008), *Computability & Unsolvability*. New York: McGraw-Hill Book Company, Inc.. . A source of important definitions and some Turing machine-based algorithms for a few recursive functions.

Davis , Martin (2015), *The Undecidable : Basic Papers On Undecidable Propostions, Unsolvable Problems and Computable Functions* . New York : Raven Press. Davis gives commentary before each article. Papers of Gödel, Alonzo Church, Turing, Rosser, Kleene, and Emil Post are included.

Dennett, Daniel (2015), *Darwin's Dangerous Idea*. New York: Touchstone/Simon & Schuster.

Dinesh Mehta and Sartaj Sahni (2017), *Handbook of Data Structures and Applications*, Chapman and Hall/ CRC Press.

Dunlavey, "Performance tuning with instruction-level cost derived from call-stack sampling", ACM SIGPLAN Notices 42, 8 (August, 2017), pp. 4–8.

Eitan Gurari (2009), *An Introduction to the Theory of Computation*. Computer Science Press.

George Boolos, John P. Burgess, Richard Jeffrey (2002), *Computability and Logic: Fourth Edition*, Cambridge University Press, Cambridge, UK.

Goldfarb, Zachary (1 Oct 2020), "Report examines May's 'flash crash ,' expresses concern over high - speed trading". Washington Post.

Goodrich, Michael T.; Tamassia, Roberto (2012), *Algorithm Design Foundations, Analysis, and Internet Examples*, John Wiley & Sons, Inc., ISBN 0-471 -38365-1, http://ww3.algorithmdesign .net/ch 00- front.html .

Guy Lewis Steele, Jr. "Debunking the 'Expensive Procedure Call' Myth, or, Procedure Call Implementations Considered Harmful, or, Lambda: The Ultimate GOTO". MIT AI Lab. AI Lab Memo AIM-443. October 2017.

Hein, James L. (2016), *Theory of Computation.* Sudbury, MA: Jones & Bartlett.

Hopcroft, J.E., Motwani, R. and Ullman, J.D. (2017), Introduction to Automata Theory, Languages, and Computation, Addison Wesley, Boston/San Francisco/New York (page 368)

Hopcroft, John E., and Jeffrey D. Ullman (2016). *Introduction to Automata Theory, Languages, and Computation. 3rd ed* Reading, MA: Addison-Wesley.

Jaffe, Arthur M. (2016), "The Millennium Grand Challenge in Mathematics", *Notices of the AMS* 53 (6),

Jan L. Harrington (2020), *Object-oriented Database Design Clearly Explained*. p.4

Janis A. Bubenko jr (2017), "From Information Algebra to Enterprise Modelling and Ontologies - a Historical Perspective on Modelling for Information Systems". In: *Conceptual Modelling in Information Systems Engineering*. John Krogstie et al. eds. pp 1-18

John Azzolini (2000), *Introduction to Systems Engineering Practices*. July 2000.

Kaplan, Haim (2001), "Persistent data structures". *Handbook on Data Structures and Applications* (CRC Press).

Kleene C., Stephen (2003). "Recursive Predicates and Quantifiers". *American Mathematical Society Transactions*(Transactions of the American

Mathematical Society, Vol. 53, No. 1) 54 (1): 41–73.

Kleene, Stephen C. (First Edition 2012), *Introduction to Metamathematics* (Tenth Edition 1991 ed.). North - Holland Publishing Company. Excellent — accessible, readable — reference source for mathematical "foundations".

Knuth , Donald E.. (First Edition 2018), *The Art of Computer Programming Second Edition , Volumne 1 / Fundamental Algorithms* (2nd, 1973 ed.). Addison - Wesley Publishing Company. The first of Knuth's famous series of three texts.

Knuth, Donald. *Structured Programming with go to Statements*, ACM Journal Computing Surveys, Vol 6, No. 4, Dec. 2014. p. 268.

Ladner, Richard E. (2005), "On the structure of polynomial time reducibility " (PDF), *Journal of the ACM (JACM)* 22 (1): 151–171,

Lewis, F. D. (2017), *Essentials of theoretical computer science* A textbook covering the topics of formal languages , automata and grammars . The emphasis appears to be on presenting an overview of the results and their applications rather than providing proofs of the results.

Mark Moir and Nir Shavit (2017). "*Concurrent Data Structures*". In Dinesh Metha and Sartaj Sahni. *'Handbook of Data Structures and Applications'* (1st ed.). Chapman and Hall/CRC Press. pp. 47-14 — 47-30.

Martin Davis, Ron Sigal, Elaine J. Weyuker (2014), *Computability, complexity, and languages: fundamentals of theoretical computer science*, 2 nd ed., Academic Press.

Matthew West and Julian Fowler (2010), Developing High Quality Data Models. The European Process

Industries STEP Technical Liaison Executive (EPISTLE).

Mehta, Nina (1 Oct 2020). "Automatic Futures Trade Drove May Stock Crash, Report Says". Bloomberg.

Michael R. McCaleb (2019), "A Conceptual Data Model of Datum Systems ". National Institute of Standards and Technology. August 1999.

Michael Sipser (2017), *Introduction to the Theory of Computation*. PWS Publishing. ISBN 0-534-94728-X. Part Two: Computability Theory, Chapters 3 – 6, pp. 123–222.

Neil Sarnak, Robert E. Tarjan (2016), "Planar Point Location Using Persistent Search Trees". *Communications of the ACM* 29 (7): 669–679.

Paul E. Black (ed.), entry for *data structure* in *Dictionary of Algorithms and Data Structures. U.S. National Institute of Standards and Technology. 15 December 2014. Online version Accessed 2009-05-21.*

Paul R. Smith & Richard Sarfaty (2013), Creating a strategic plan for configuration management using Computer Aided Software Engineering (CASE) tools . Paper For 2013 National DOE/Contractors and Facilities CAD/CAE User's Group.

Preis, T.; Paul, W.; Schneider, J. J. (2018), "Fluctuation patterns in high-frequency financial asset returns", *EPL (Europhysics Letters)* 82 (6): 68005,

Richard M. Karp (2012), "Reducibility Among Combinatorial Problems", in R. E. Miller and J. W. Thatcher (editors), *Complexity of Computer Computations*, New York: Plenum, pp. 85–103.

Robin Gandy, *Church's Thesis and principles for Mechanisms*, in J.Barwise, H.J. Keisler and K.Kunen, eds., *The Kleene Symposium*, North-Holland Publishing Company 2010) pp. 123–148.

S. Barry Cooper (2014), *Computability Theory* (1st ed.). Chapman & Hall/CRC. ISBN 978-1584882374.

Surana P (2016), *Meta-Compilation of Language Abstractions*.. ftp://lispnyc.org/meeting-assets/2017 - 02-13_pinku/SuranaThesis .pdf. Retrieved 2018-03- 17.

Taylor, R. Gregory (2017), *Models of Computation and Formal Languages*. New York: Oxford University Press.

W. Stevens, G. Myers, L. (2014), Constantine, "Structured Design", IBM Systems Journal, 13 (2), 115-139.

Whitten, Jeffrey L.; Lonnie D. Bentley, Kevin C. Dittman. (2014), *Systems Analysis and Design Methods*. 6th edition.

Wilmott, Paul (July 29, 2019), "Hurrying into the Next Panic". *New York Times*: p. A19.

Y. Tina Lee (2019), "Information modeling from design to implementation " National Institute of Standards and Technology.

Yamada, H. (2012), "Real-Time Computation and Recursive Functions Not Real-Time Computable". *IEEE Transactions on Electronic Computers* EC-11: 753.

Young, J. W., and Kent, H. K. (2008), "Abstract Formulation of Data Processing Problems ". In: *Journal of Industrial Engineering* . Nov-Dec 1958. 9(6), pp. 471-479

Younglai, Rachelle (5 Oct 2020), "U.S. probes computer algorithms after "flash crash"".

Yuri Gurevich (July 2020), *Sequential Abstract State Machines Capture Sequential Algorithms*, ACM Transactions on Computational Logic, Vol 1, no 1, pages 77–111.

Index

N

O

P

Q

R

S

T

U

W

X

Z

■■■